The Views Are Worth It

Photography and Poetry Collection

Annie K David

ISBN-13: [978-1-7356720-0-7]

Library of Congress Control Number: 2020916891

Printed in the United States of America

Special Thanks:

I want to thank the woman who always allowed and encouraged me to feel. So, here's a thank you to you, Mom. You have let me feel every emotion, and not once did you make me feel bad for feeling. The world is a tough place, but you make it so much easier. Thank you for rubbing my head when I cry, and for giving me hugs when you notice me getting grumpy. Thank you for supporting my journey every step of the way. The love and support you show me encourages me every day. You are my inspiration.

Thank you to my best friend and loving fiancé, Damon. I appreciate all the love, support, and kindness you continuously show me. Thank you for being patient with me and for reminding me to enjoy life. I love you more than you know.

I would also like to thank everyone else who has been in my life. Every single one of you helped me become the person I am today. An extra special thanks to all the people who stood by my side when the going got tough and loved me when I needed it most.

(Especially: Aly, CarolAnne, Cec, Jenni, Hailie, Jojo, and Alayna.)

Each of these poems was written during a distinctly emotional time in my life, and they were written between the ages of 16 and 21. I have felt an abundance of feelings, and I plan to continue feeling. Don't forget, feeling is healthy. Feeling is strengthening. Feeling isn't wrong. So here are poems from the deepest parts of my soul. Here is me… feeling.

Between each chapter are photographs to offer you a moment of peace. Take a deep breath and enjoy

I'll see you on the other side.

Notice*: When revising my poems, I realized I didn't feel the same way I did when I initially wrote them; however, I needed to feel those feelings to grow. So, I kept the poems and added edits under a few of them. Feeling helps you grow.

Contents

Love

Love comes in many forms,

but so does evil.

What we had wasn't love,

but we sure as hell tried to pretend it

was.

Growing up is realizing love isn't enough in relationships.

You need effort,

      communication,

                time,

and so much more.

But I do wish love were enough.

He only loves you when he wants to,

my dear,

and that's not love.

At times, I feel too broken to be loved,

but not too broken to love,

and that's the hardest part.

Edit: I have now learned that I'm not too broken or damaged to love. The key is finding people who want to love all of you… even the broken parts. Everyone's a little bit broken, and everyone needs a whole lot of love.

Maybe he was right.

Maybe he can't give me the love I need.

Well, can't…

      or won't.

Whichever it is,

I'll always wish he was able to.

One day,

        he woke up and decided he no
longer loved me.

The next day,

        I woke up and decided to love
myself.

With how quick the love disappeared,

I wonder if it was ever there at all.

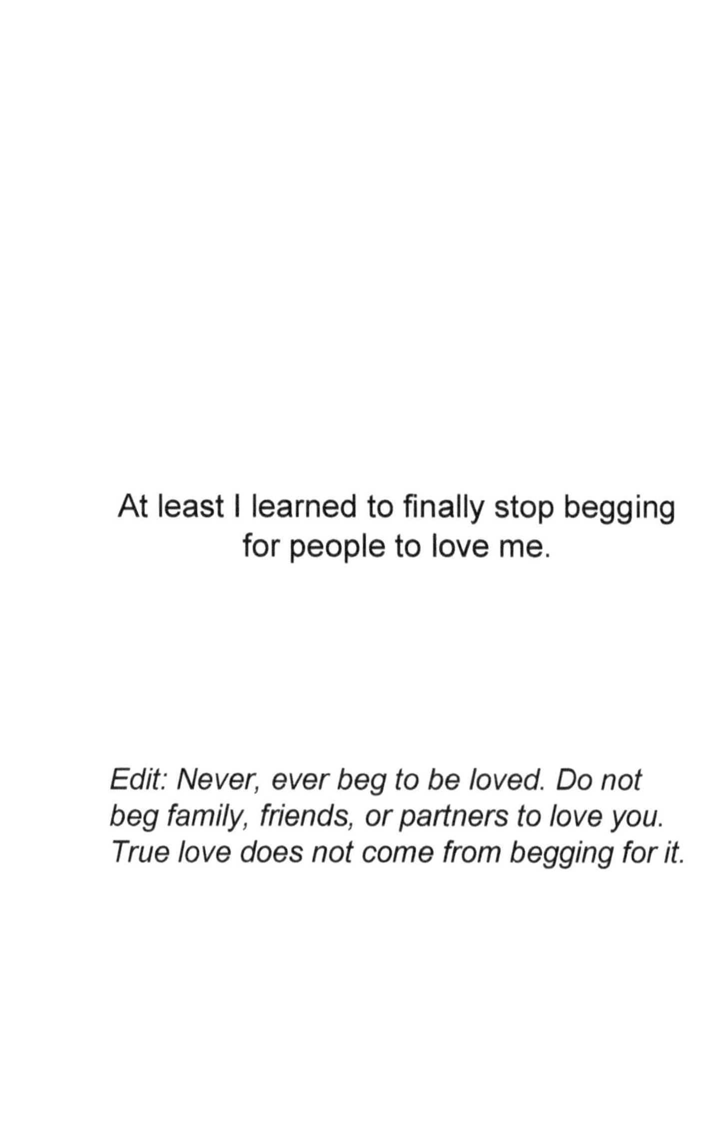

At least I learned to finally stop begging
for people to love me.

*Edit: Never, ever beg to be loved. Do not
beg family, friends, or partners to love you.
True love does not come from begging for it.*

I hope you find someone that loves you
for you,

not for the love you give them.

If they love you,

then they love you.

And if they don't,

then they don't.

You'll keep breathing either way.

I always wonder if she stopped loving
me when she put her hands around my
neck,

but it must have been before.

*Edit: A healthy reminder: people do not
leave bruises on people they love, no matter
what they may say.*

Perhaps,

the truth is that some people don't know
how to be loved.

Maybe the last process of loving is
letting go.

So,
    this is me,
                coming to an end
of loving you,
                needing to let you go.

Parents are supposed to love you,

not leave you.

I deserve more love than I've ever received.

I tend to love too much and think too less.

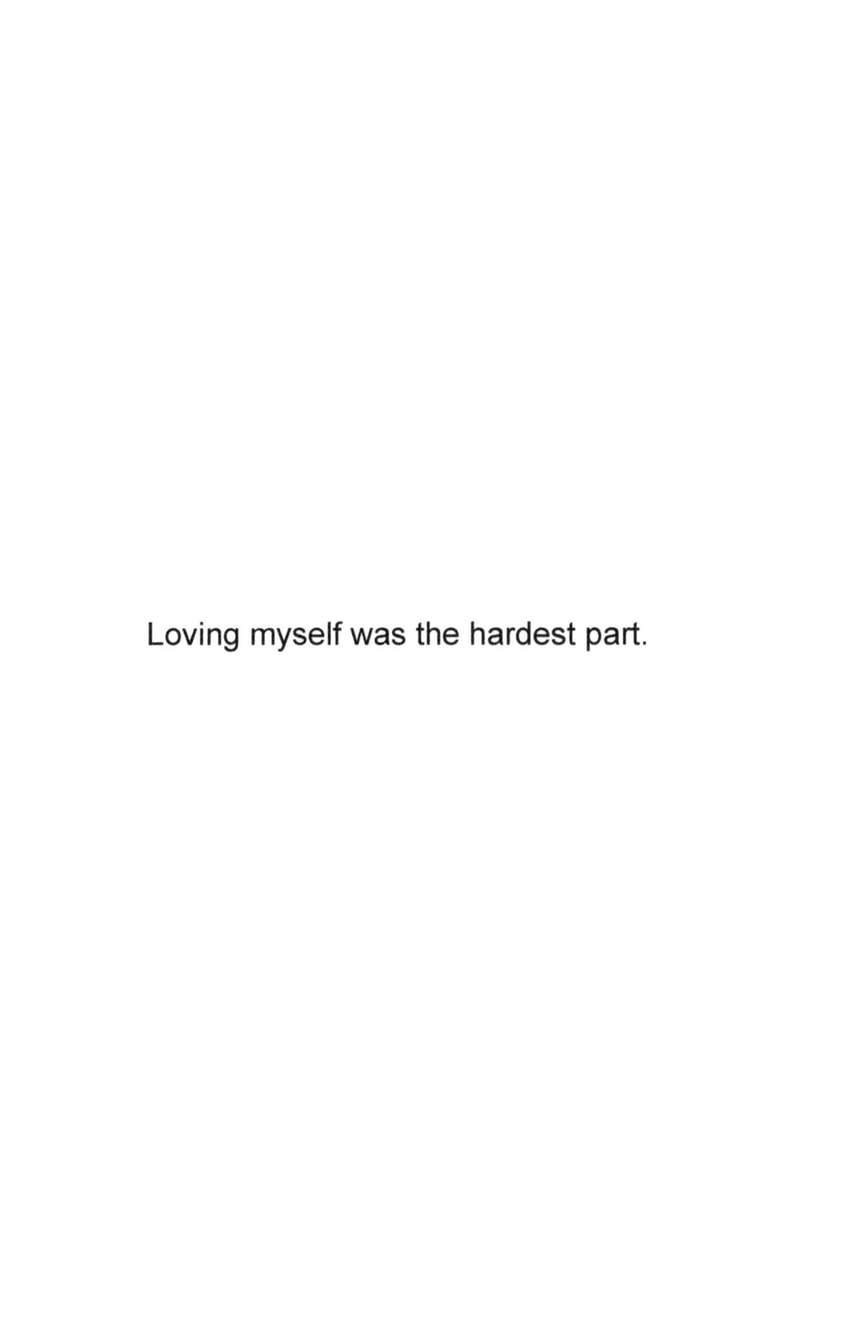

Loving myself was the hardest part.

I hope you find love in places you never
even knew it existed.

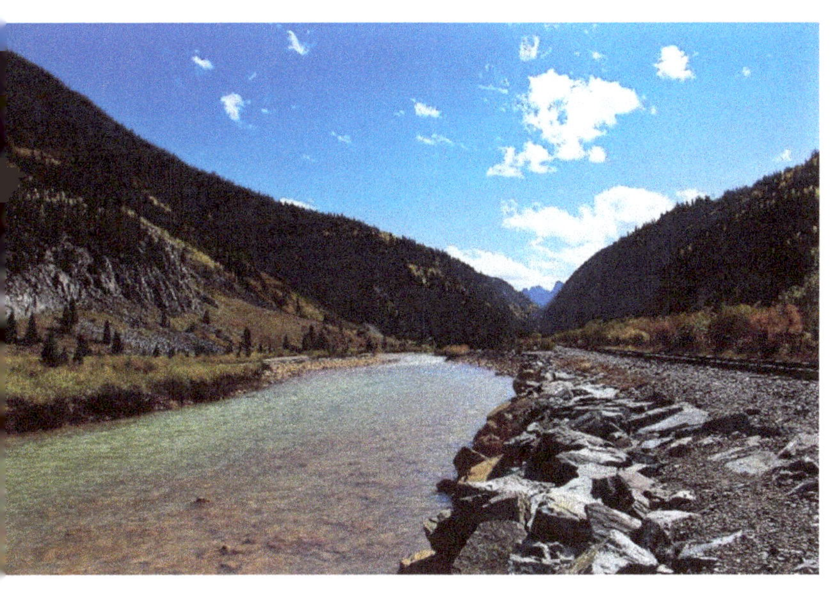

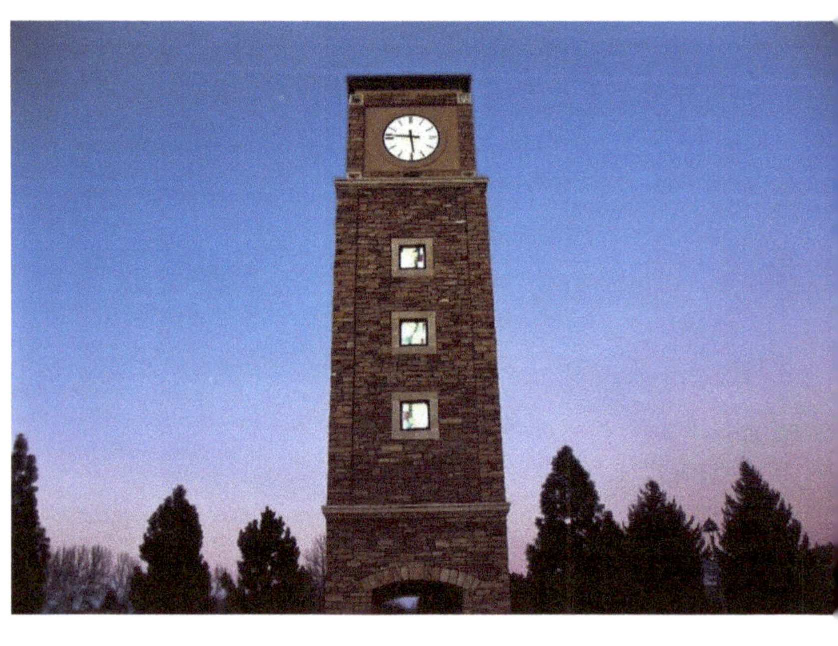

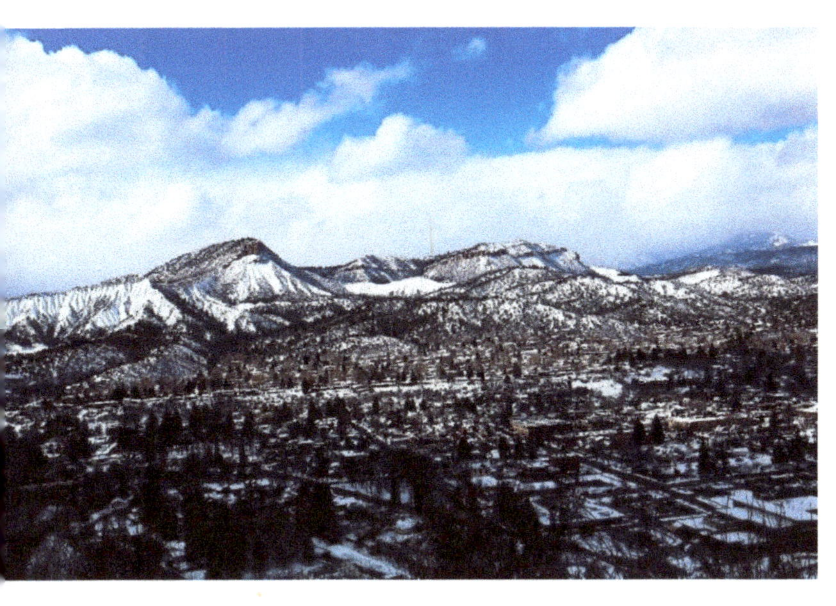

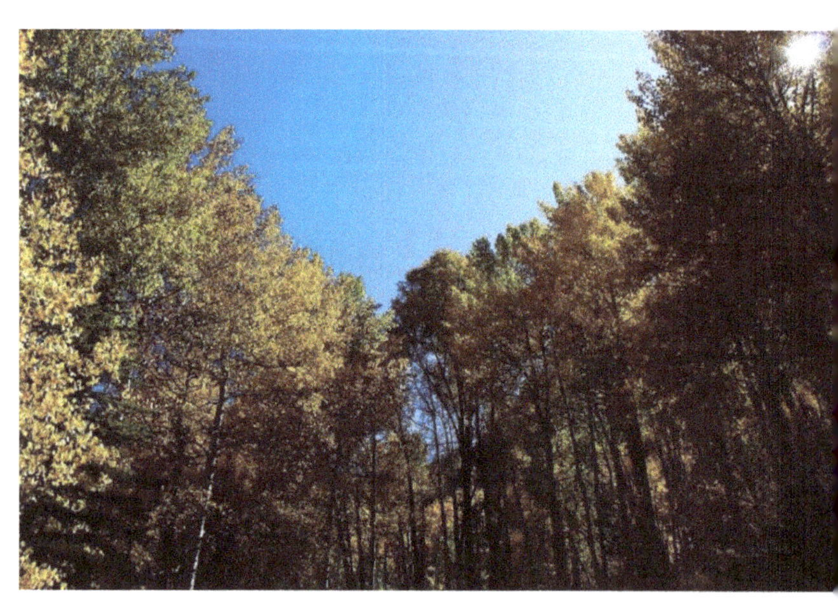

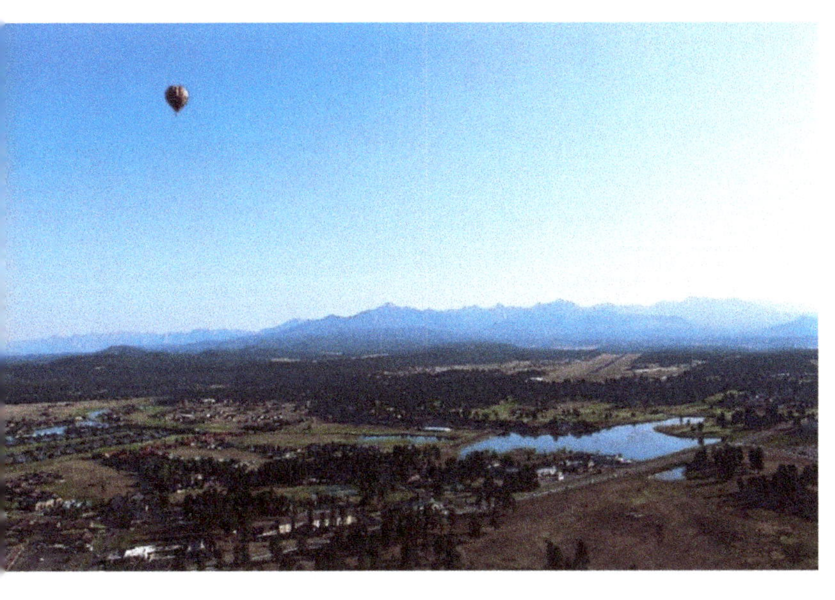

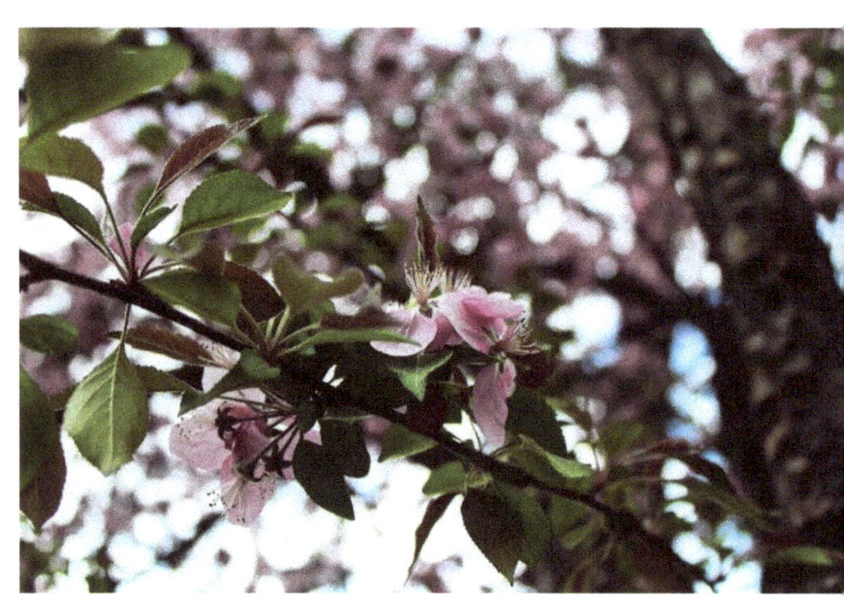

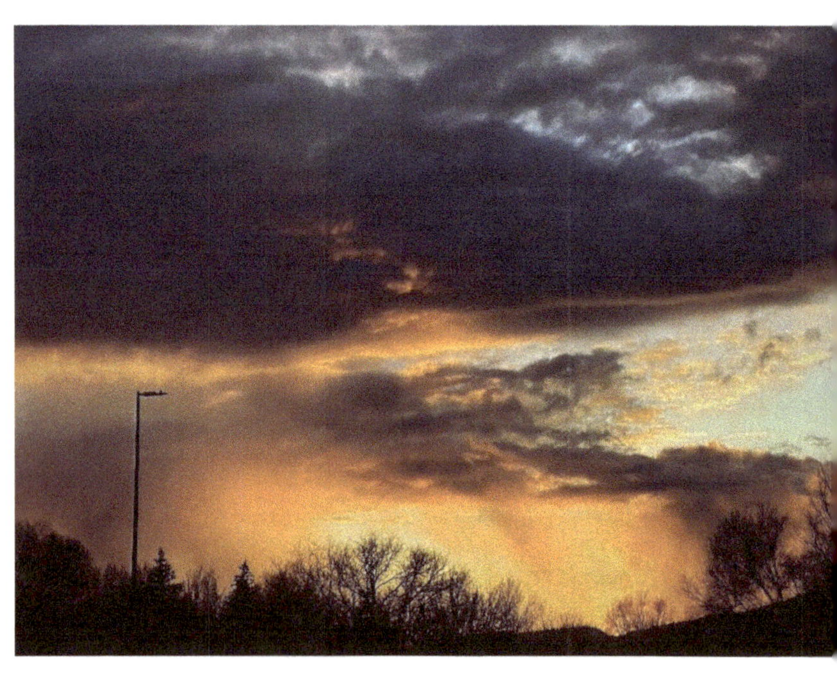

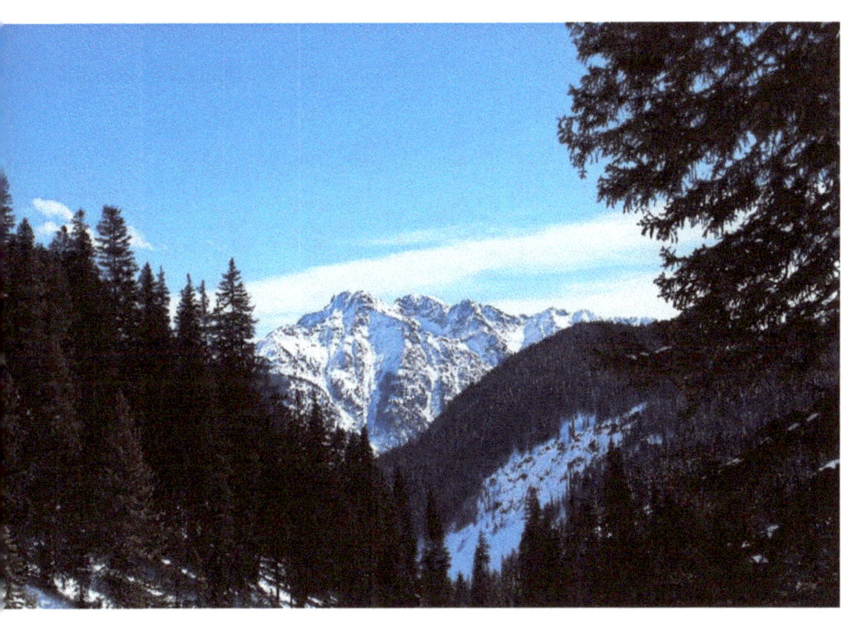

Learn

My heart hurts for the people I've lost,

but I can't let it hurt too much.

The people you lose help shape the
person you become.

There are equal forces in the universe.

Things must fall apart to fall back
together.

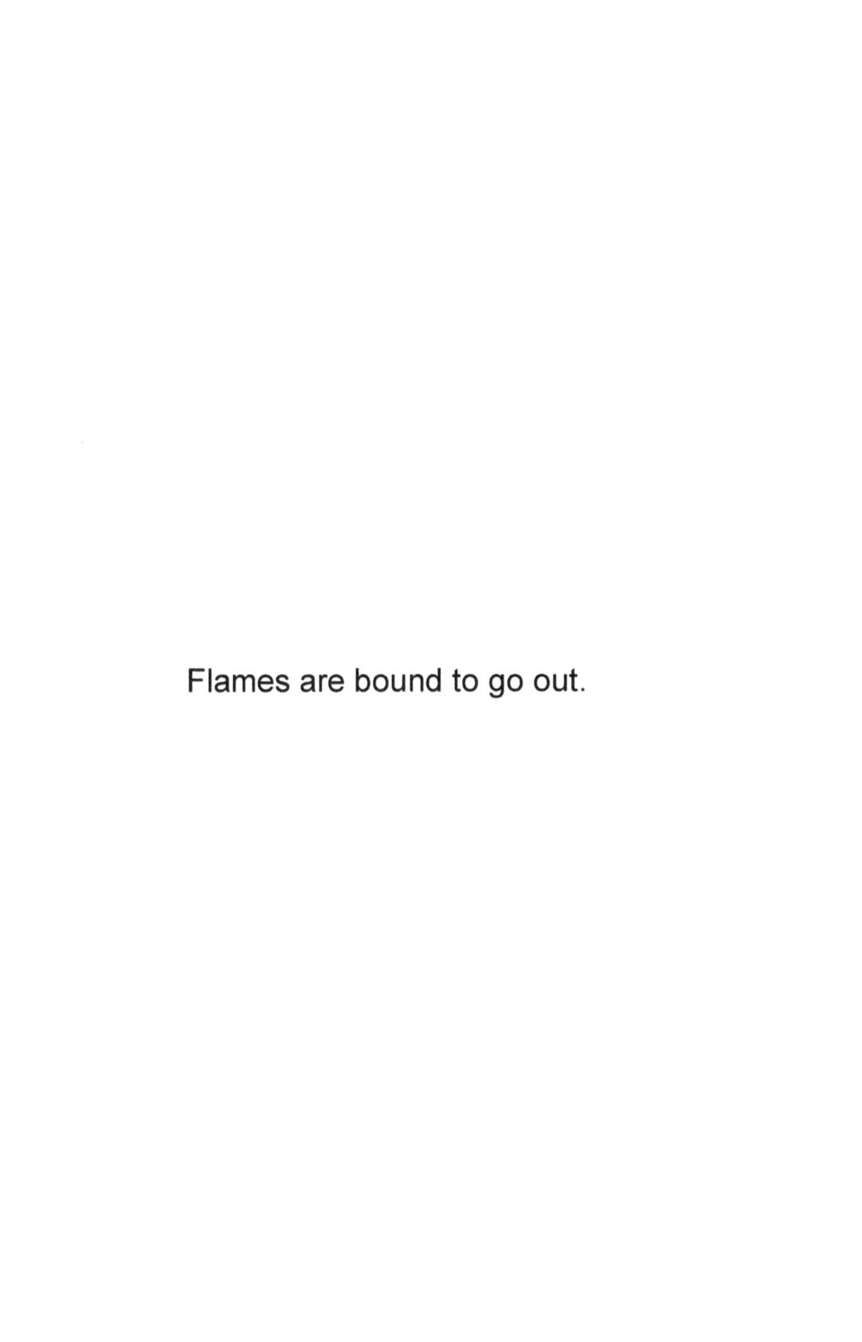

Flames are bound to go out.

Stop picking at the scab.

Stop picking the scab off.

How is it ever supposed to heal?

Stop trying to get attention from people who do not care to give you attention.

Stop picking at the scab.

Stop going back to what hurt you.

Stop pulling the scab off.

Let the hurt heal.

Nothing heals quick, especially when you keep picking at it.

Let it be.

If you're chasing them,

then that means they're running.

Begging someone not to leave doesn't
stop them from walking out the door.

Some bridges need to be burnt.

Humans can be monsters, too.

The world destroying you isn't an
excuse to destroy others.

People will constantly tear you down,

it is how you rebuild yourself that

matters.

You shouldn't drink poison just because you're thirsty.

You can't save people,

they must save themselves.

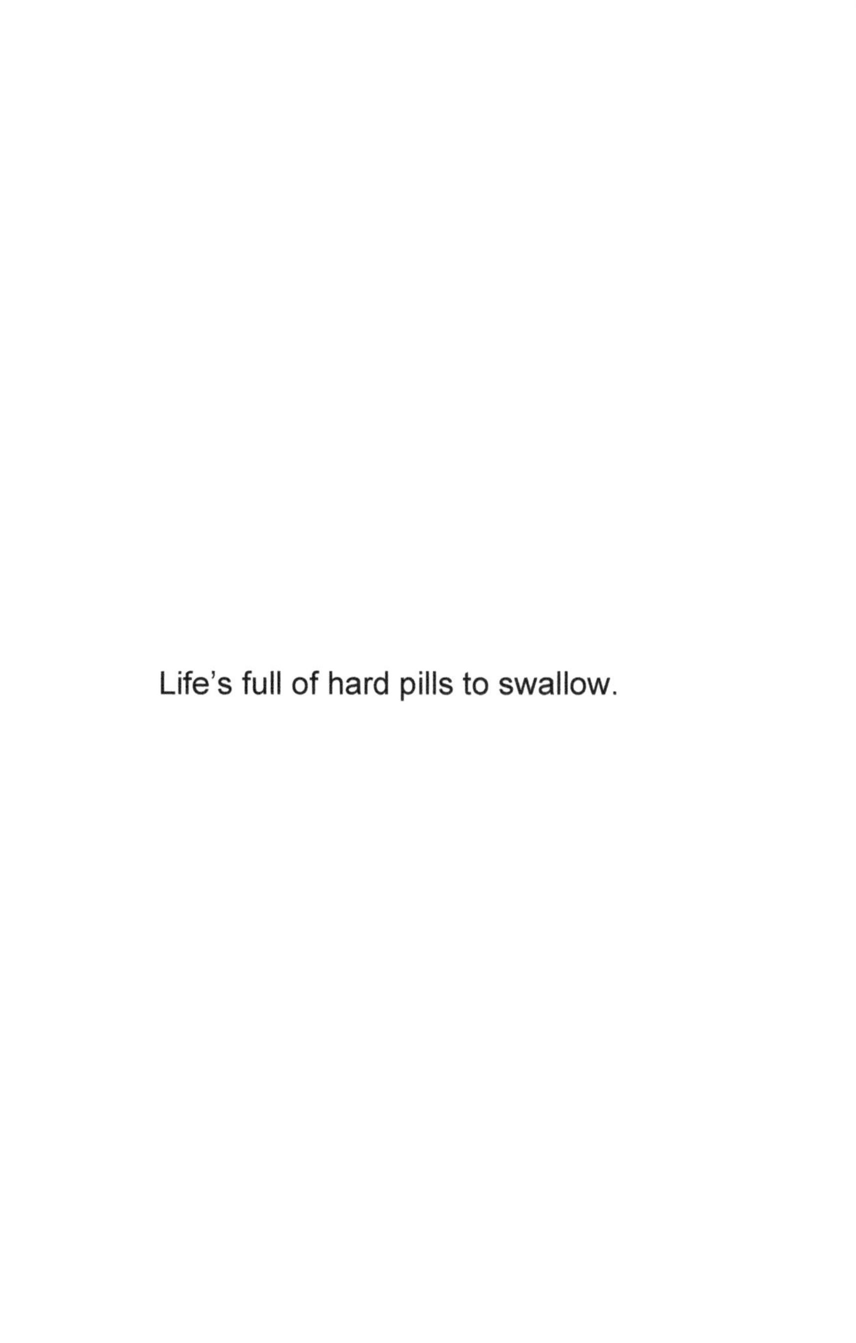

Life's full of hard pills to swallow.

The higher your horse,

the harder your fall.

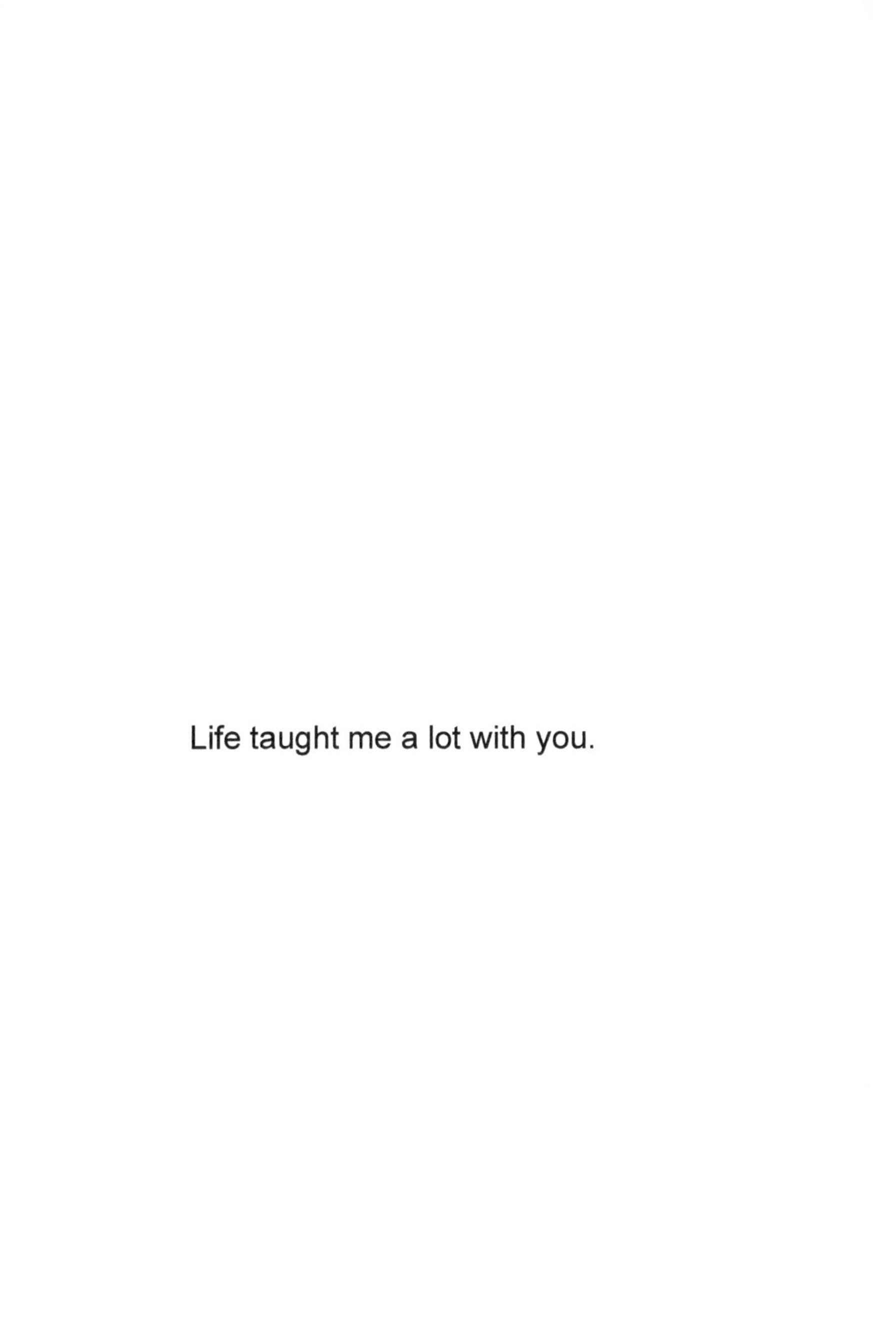

Life taught me a lot with you.

Everyone is just trying their best and
hoping that it's good enough.

If you aren't happy,

      change whatever is making you unhappy.

There are endless jobs out there.

A job should not cost you your happiness.

There are billions of people out there.

A person should not cost you your happiness.

You get one life…

      make it a happy one.

Life might not go perfect,

but from my experience,

the twisty mountain

roads have much more

to offer

than the straight ahead.

Most things happen for a reason,

some (other) things just happen.

The few months before graduating are sad.

It's like you're watching everything play out and there's nothing you can do about it.

You can't slow down time...

        but you can enjoy it.

Take a breath.

You made it.

Edit: This can also apply to the ending of anything, honestly. Endings can be sad, but new beginnings can be even more exciting.

Life will be okay.

There will be hard times.

Your heart will break.

You won't get that job you wanted.

You may barely be able to make rent.

You may feel defeated by the world.

But you aren't.

Every time life knocks you down,

                        stand up

            taller.

You love, you feel, you learn, you grow.

That's life.

Just many, many cycles of loving,
feeling, learning, and growing.

Be gentle with yourself.

No one else knows what you're going
through...

but you.

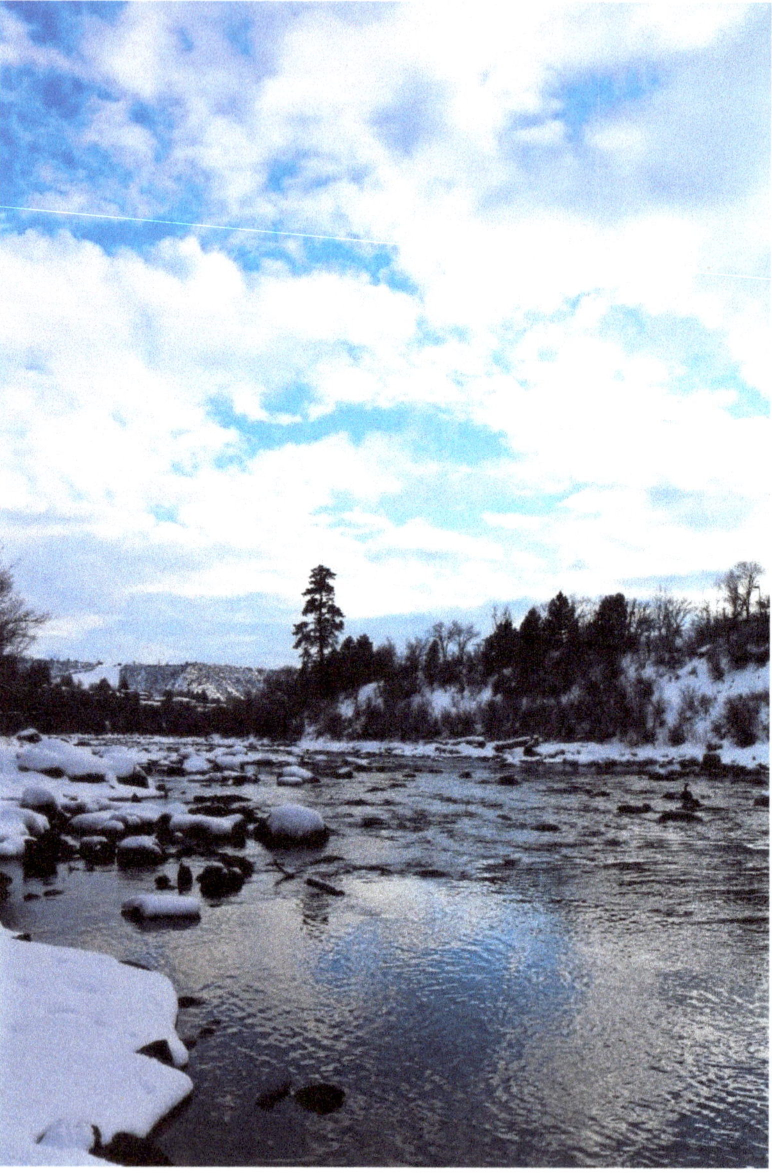

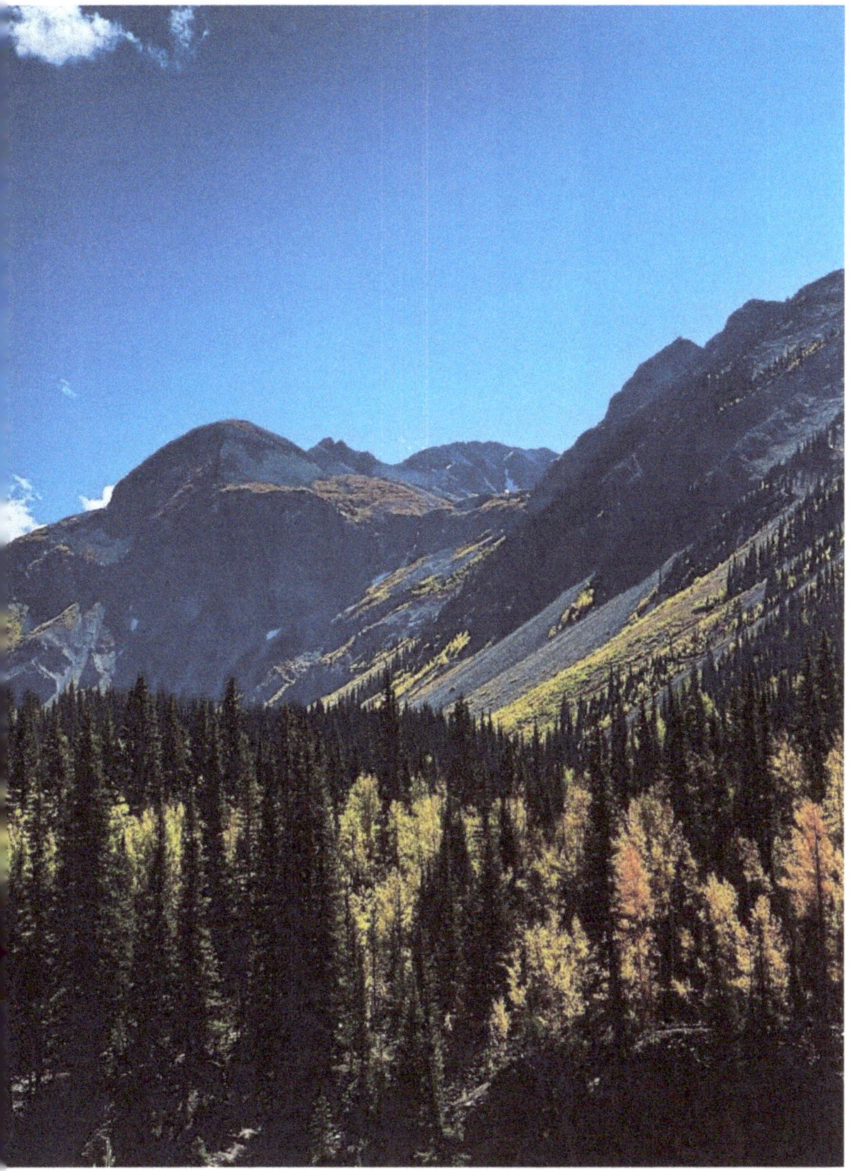

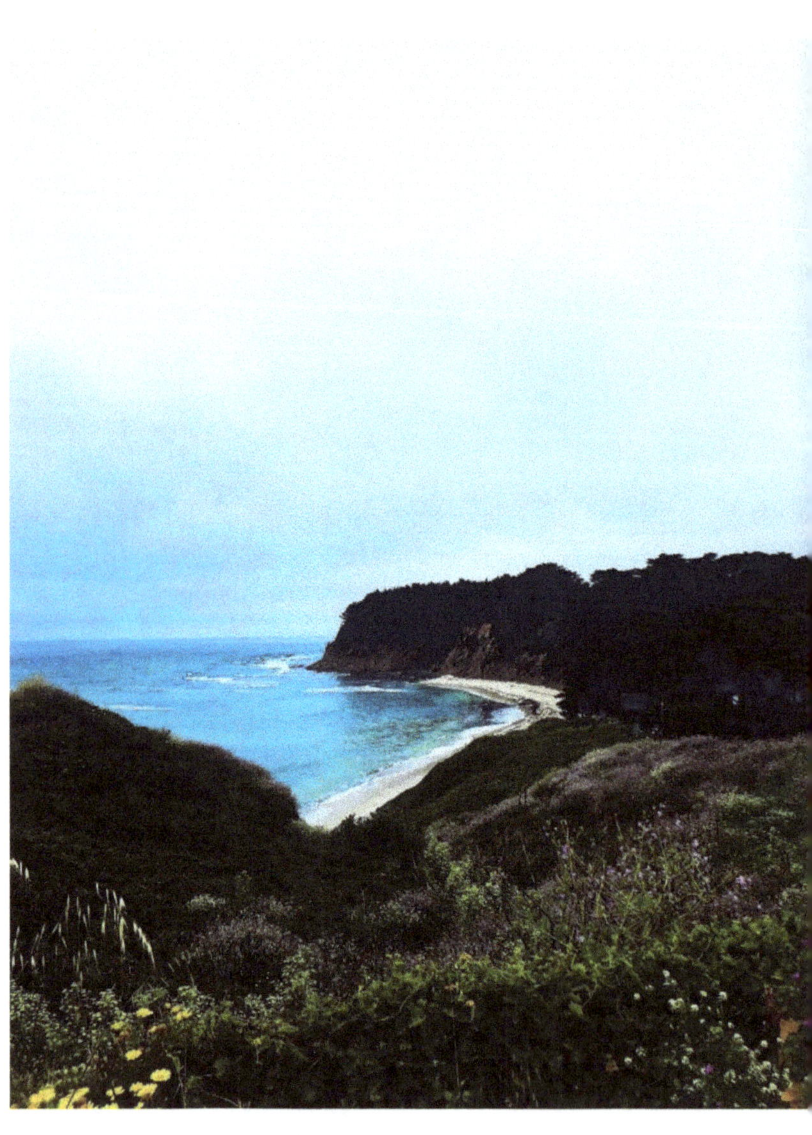

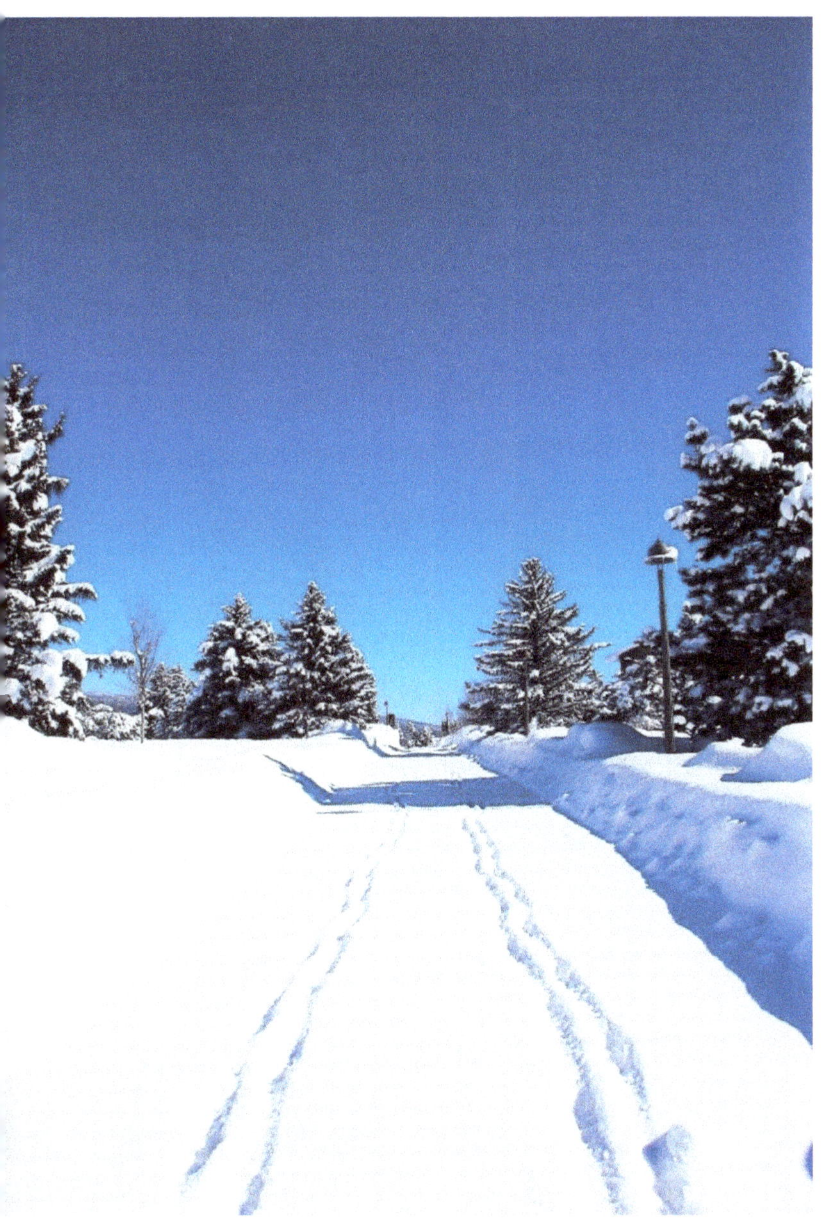

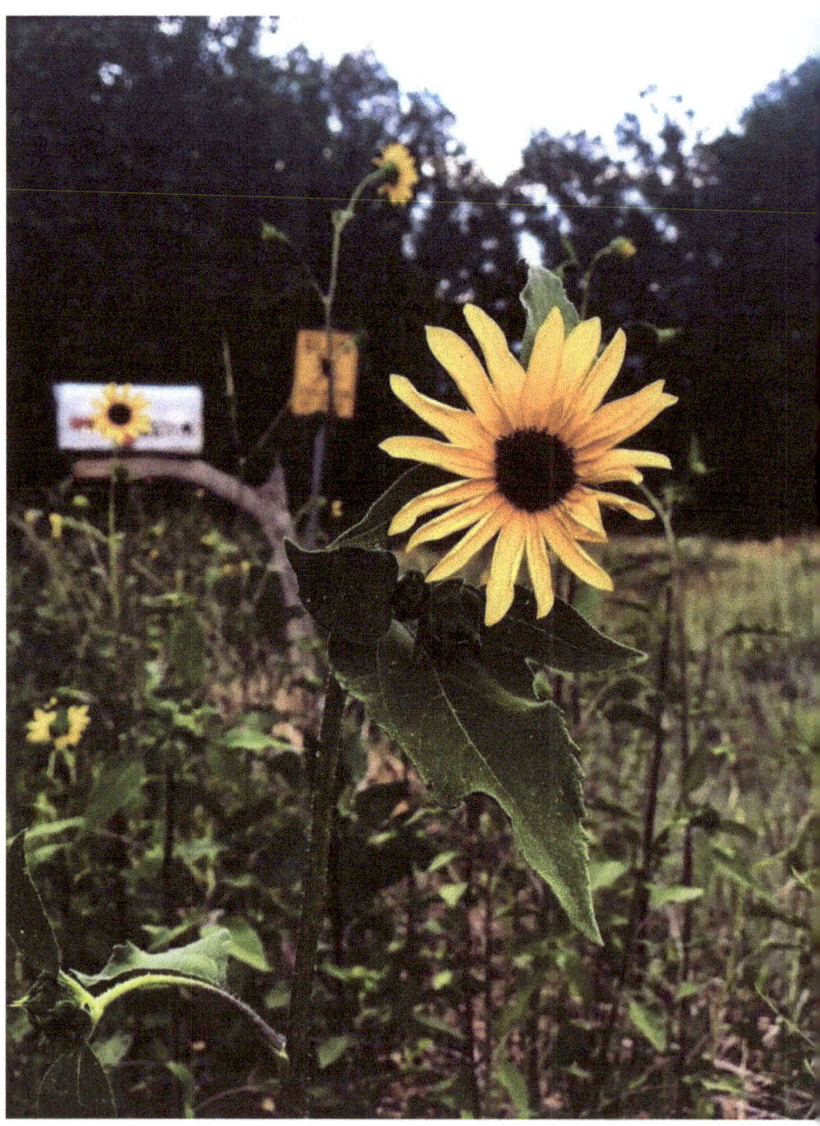

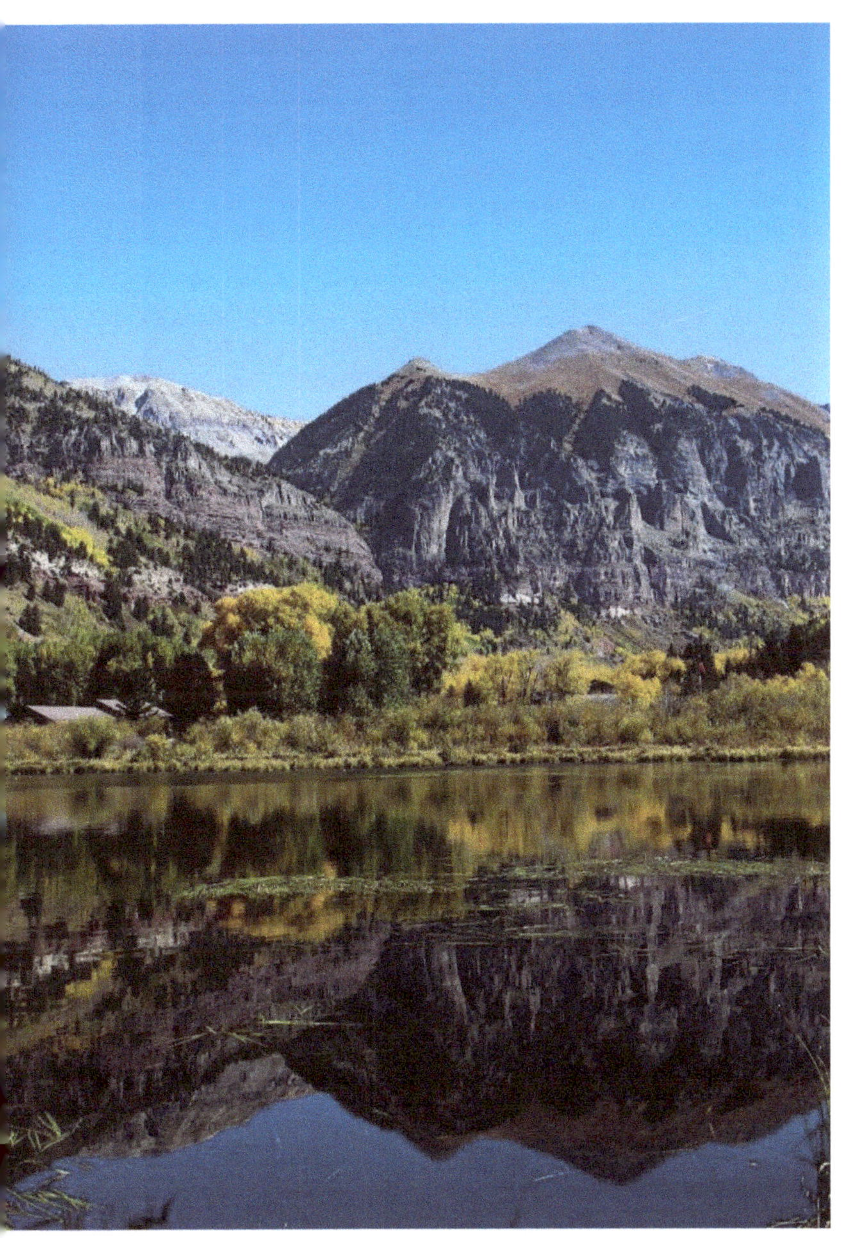

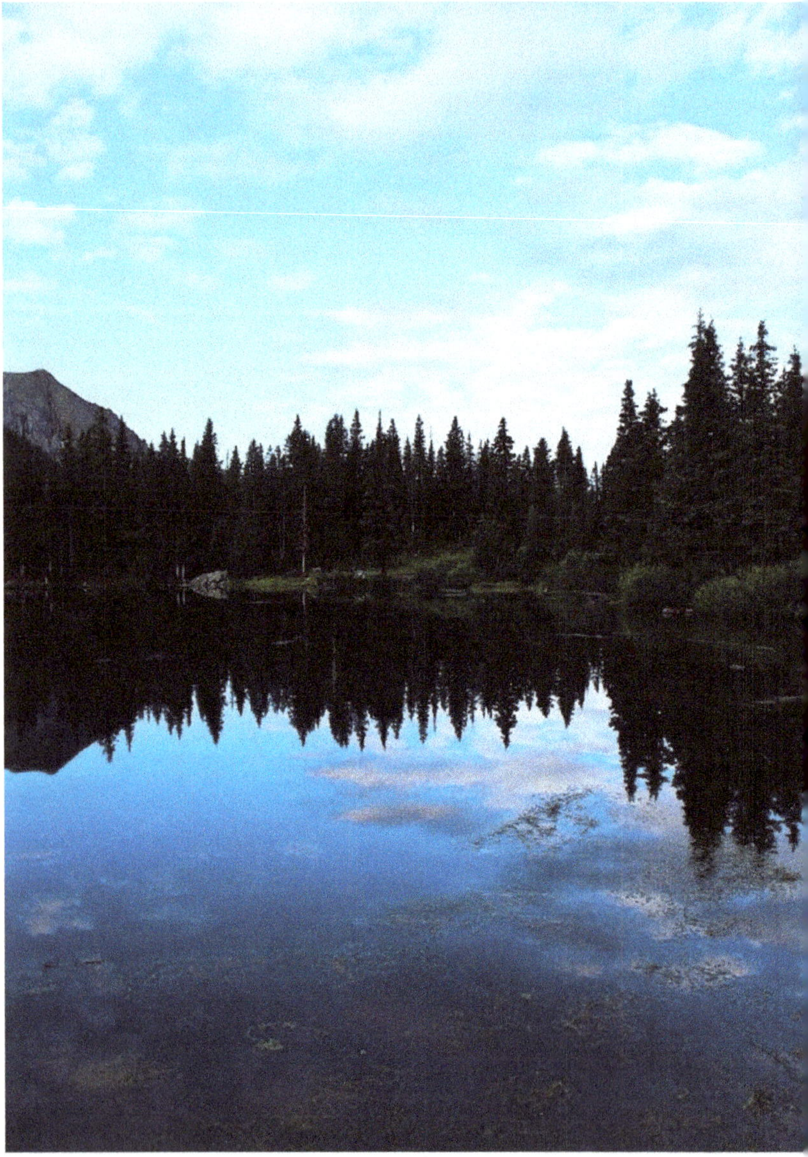

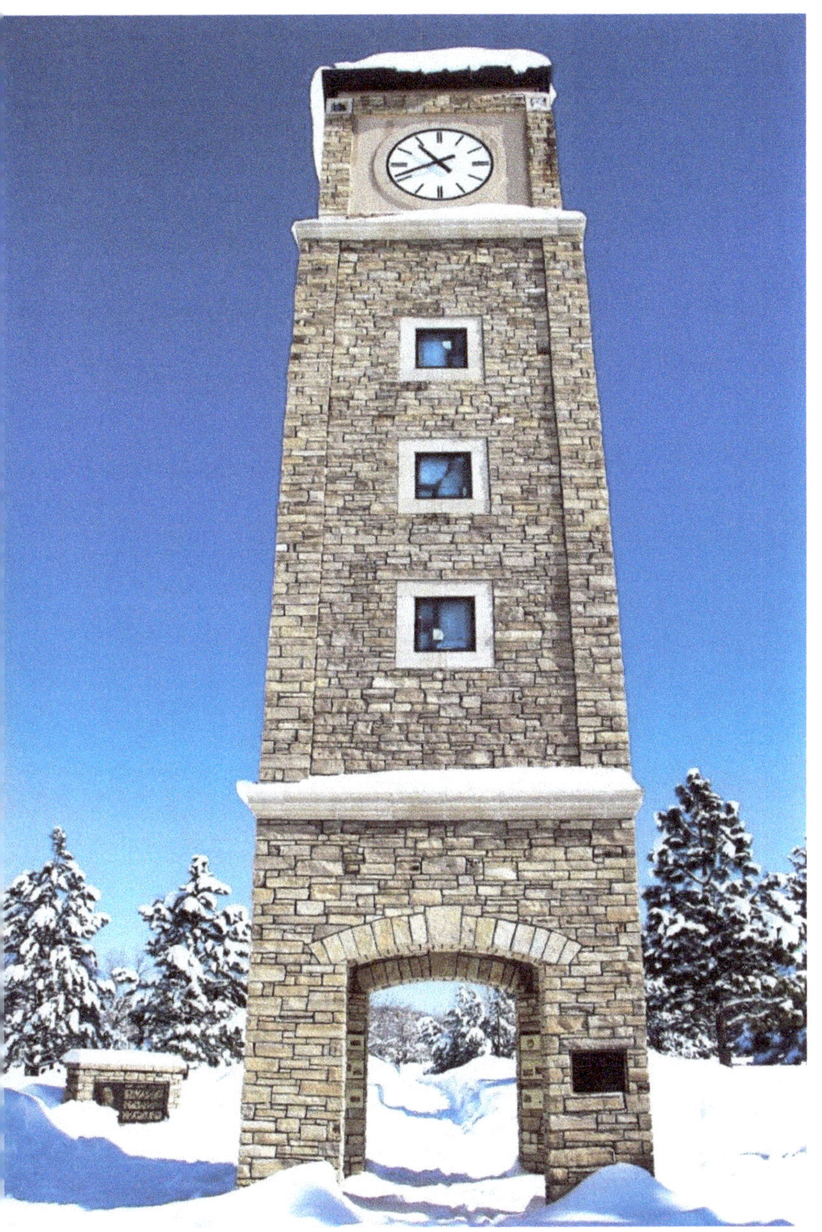

Feel

Pain has always been comfortable to
me,

a devilish sort of comfort.

You hit a point in life where you want the
monsters under the bed to get you.

The pain turns to numbness,

and the numbness turns to nothing.

It all takes time.

You think you're better,

until one little thing shows you that

you're not.

It's like fighting a monster

but knowing that you probably won't win,

so why even fight.

Edit: I wrote this poem due to being bipolar. Mental illness is exceptionally tough at times, but you must keep fighting. Build yourself an army of people who care about you; you don't have to fight alone. There are many resources out there to help you tame the monster. If you're still fighting, then you're the one winning. Never stop fighting. One day you may beat the monster, or even learn how to live peacefully with the little devil. Battles are never easy, but I promise you can win this one.

I've started to forget my father's face,

which means that,

in time,

I'll forget yours, too.

People who leave were never meant to
stay.

I deserved a better goodbye.

I don't want to be someone's cup of

tea

or cup of coffee.

I want to be someone's cup of water.

Everyone needs water.

I started finding comfort in the fact that
we were under the same sky

since it was the only thing I could find
comfort in.

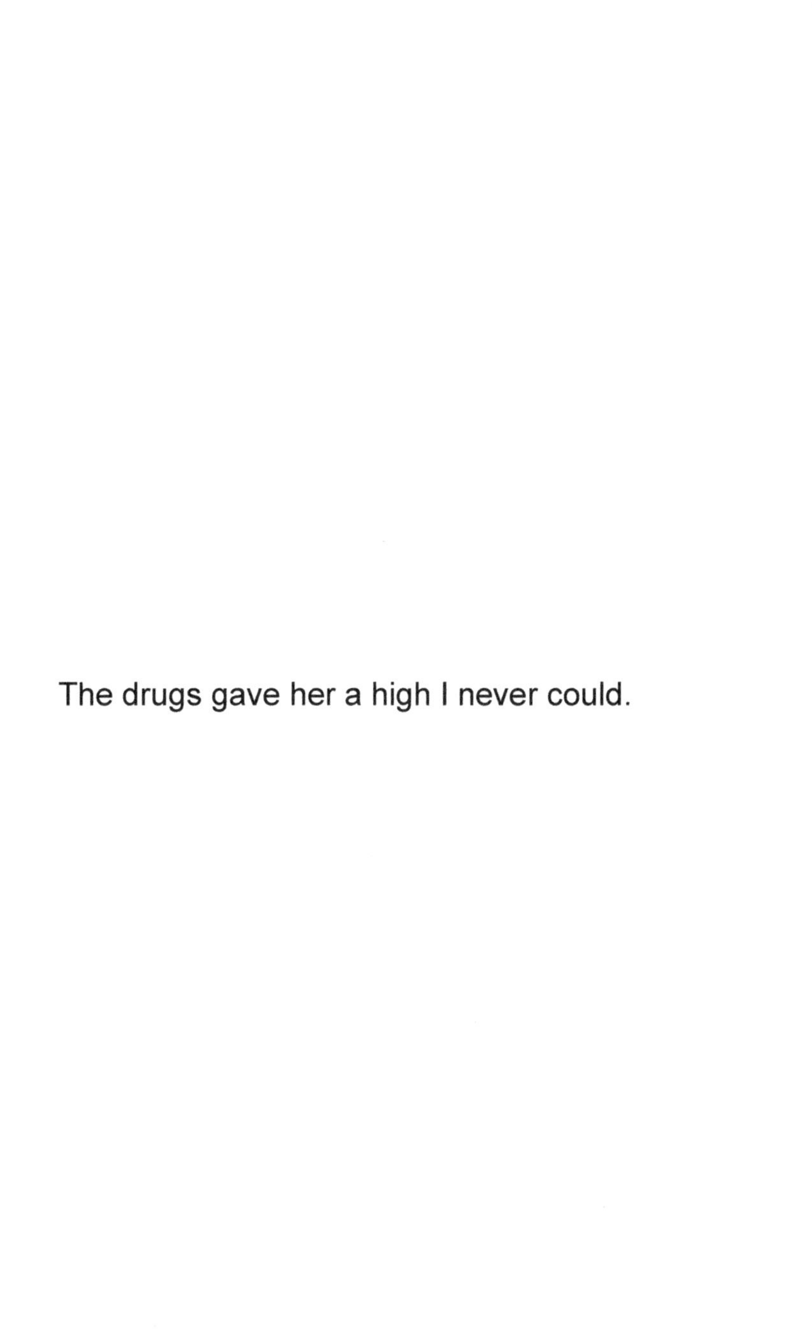

The drugs gave her a high I never could.

She cleansed her soul by manipulating mine.

Her heart wasn't a few sizes too small…

She didn't have one.

You put me through hell,

so, don't act like an angel.

I hope you never have to think about anything as much as I think about you.

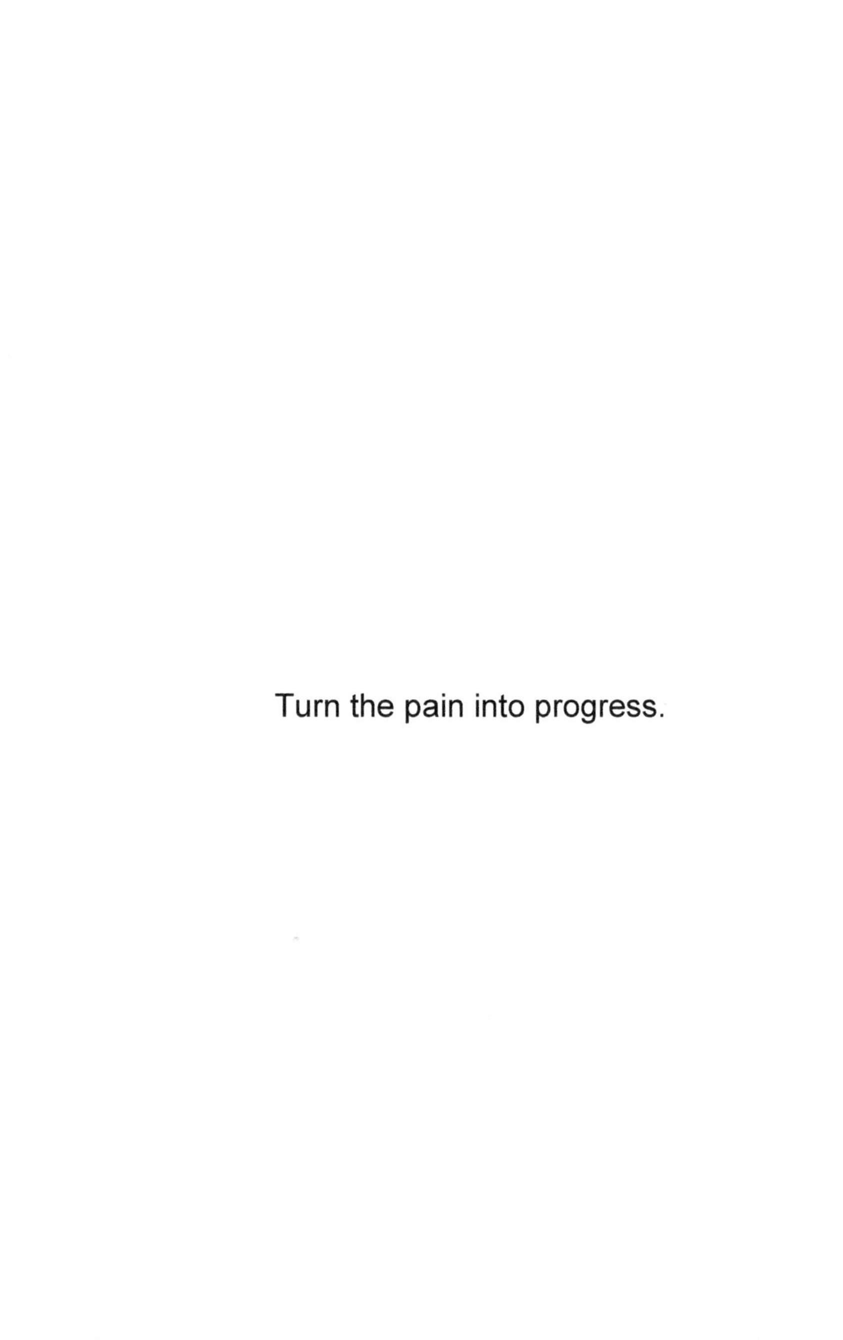
Turn the pain into progress.

I didn't wear sadness like a good fitting
coat anymore.

When it came it made me

uncomfortable and itchy,

and I wanted it off me.

That's how I knew I was getting better...
the sadness was no longer comfortable.

Maybe I'm scared to be happy because
it can be ripped away at any moment,

and there's nothing I can do about it.

Sadness, on the other hand,

is never missed,

nearly as much as happiness is,

when it's ripped from someone.

A leaky pipe is bound to burst.

Take care of yourself.

You know how it has to rain before the rainbow?

Well, I just hope my storms almost over.

Life is simultaneously precious and
painful,

so, enjoy it.

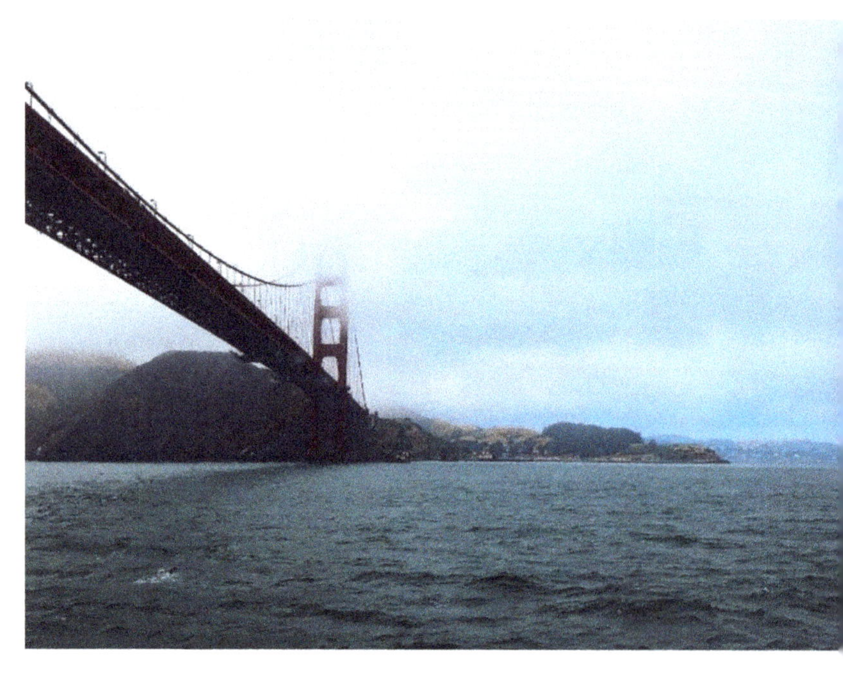

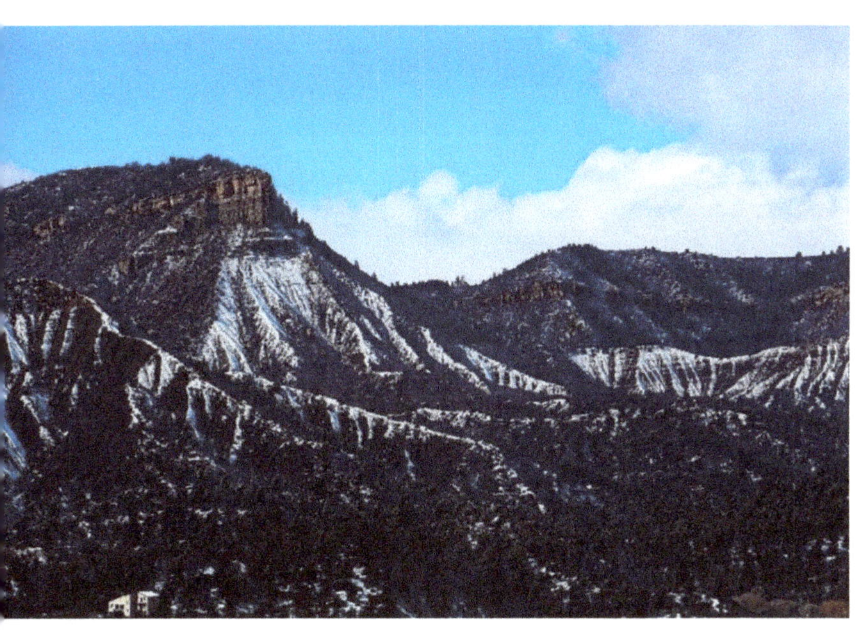

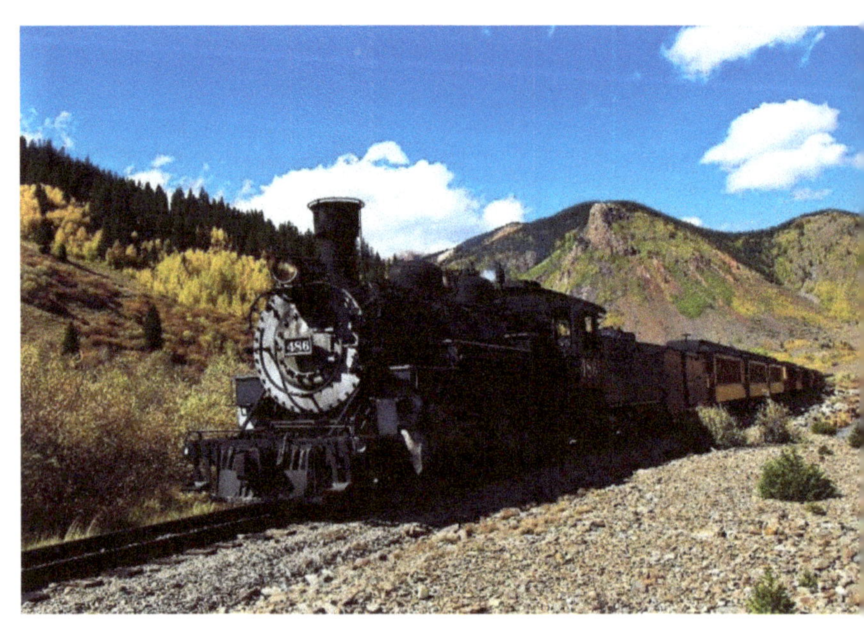

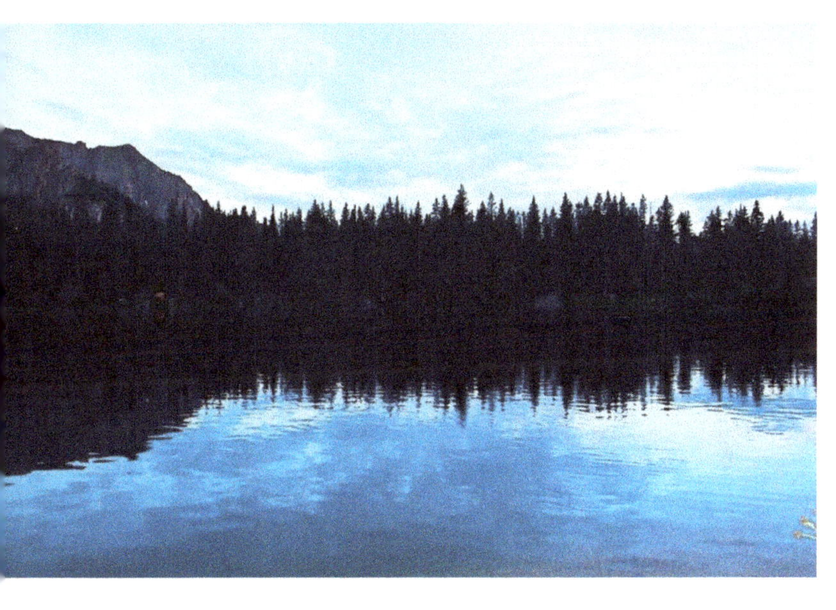

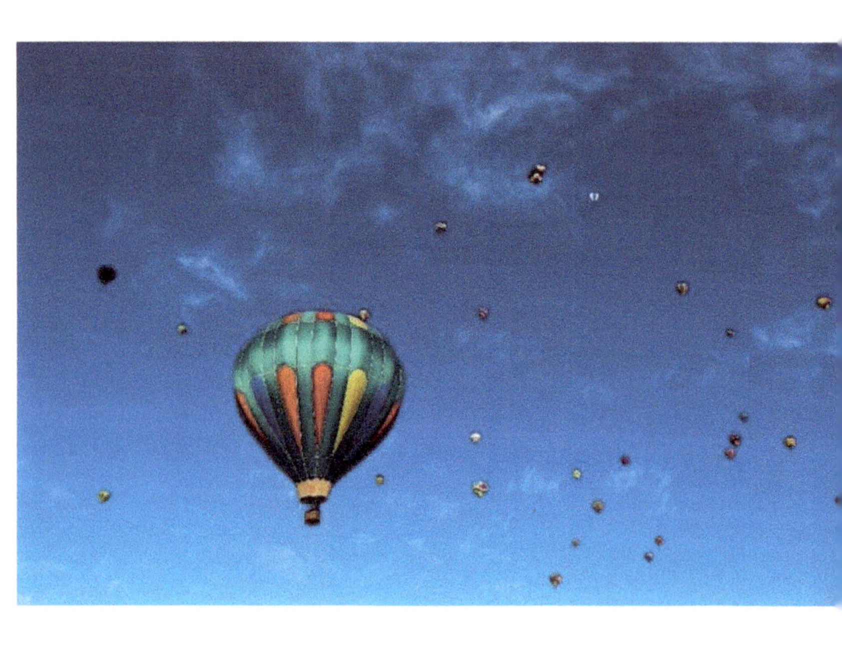

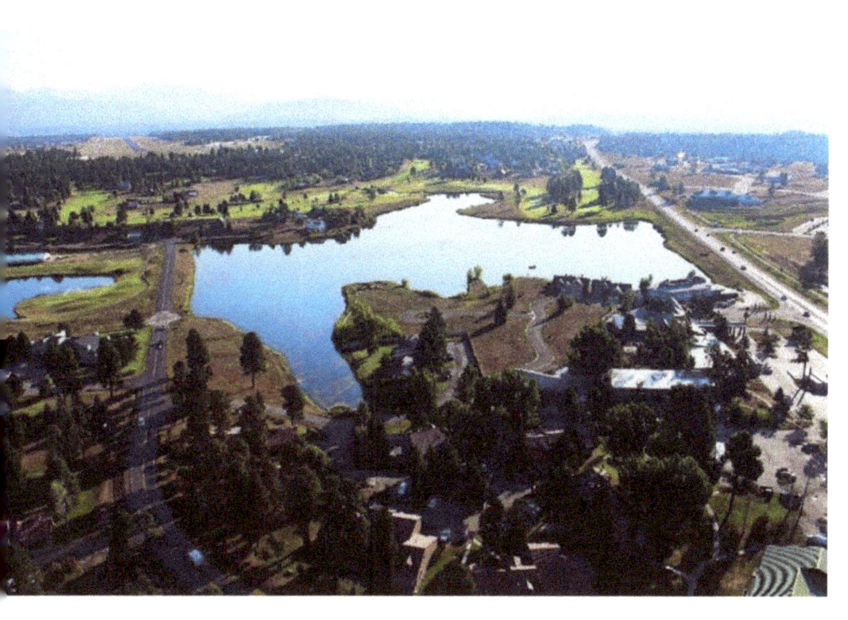

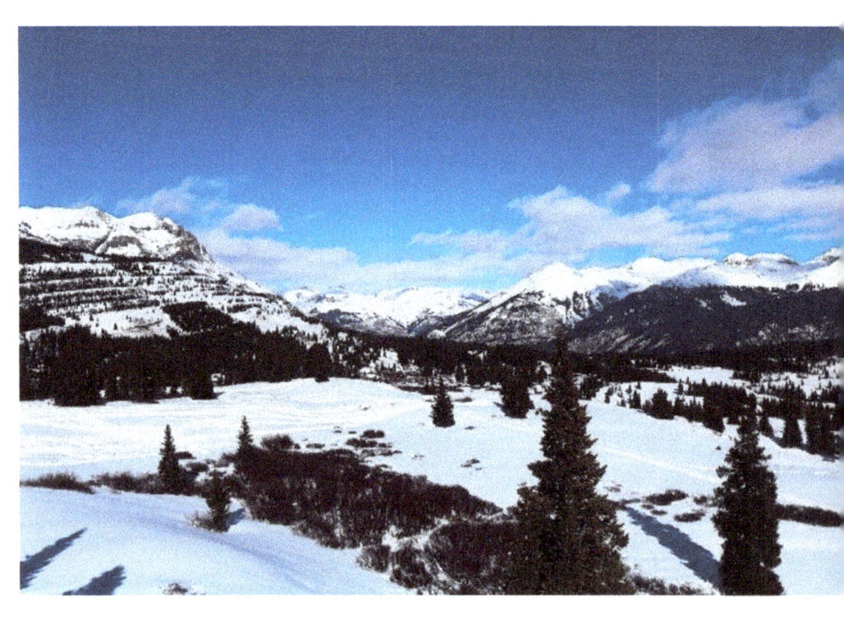

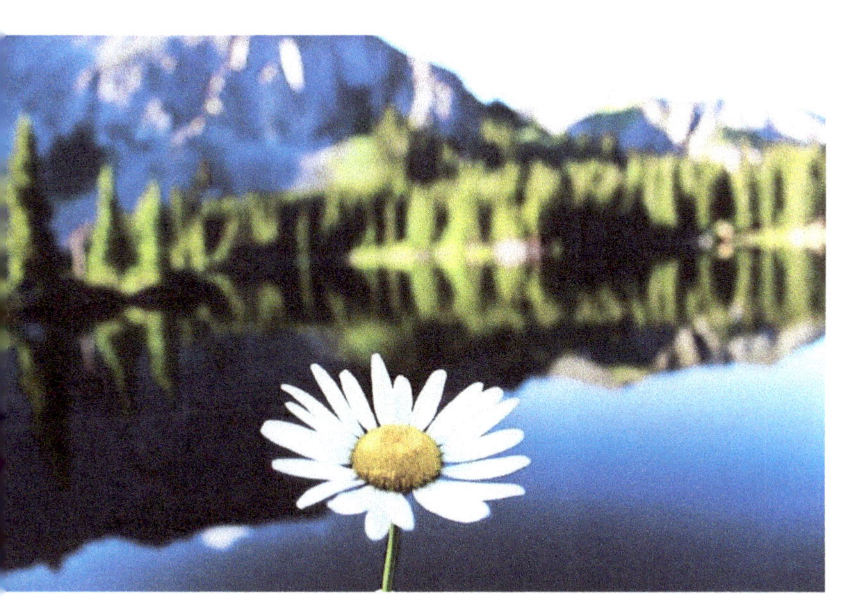

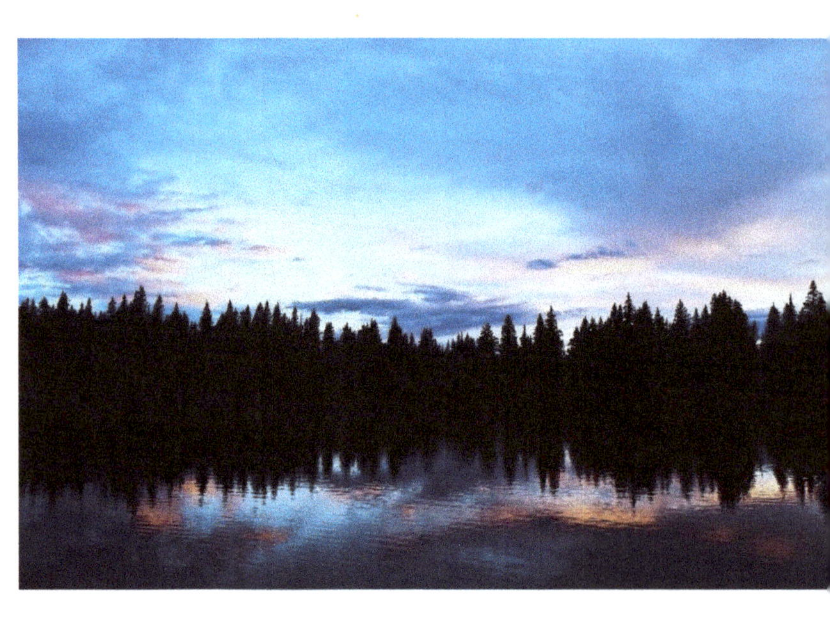

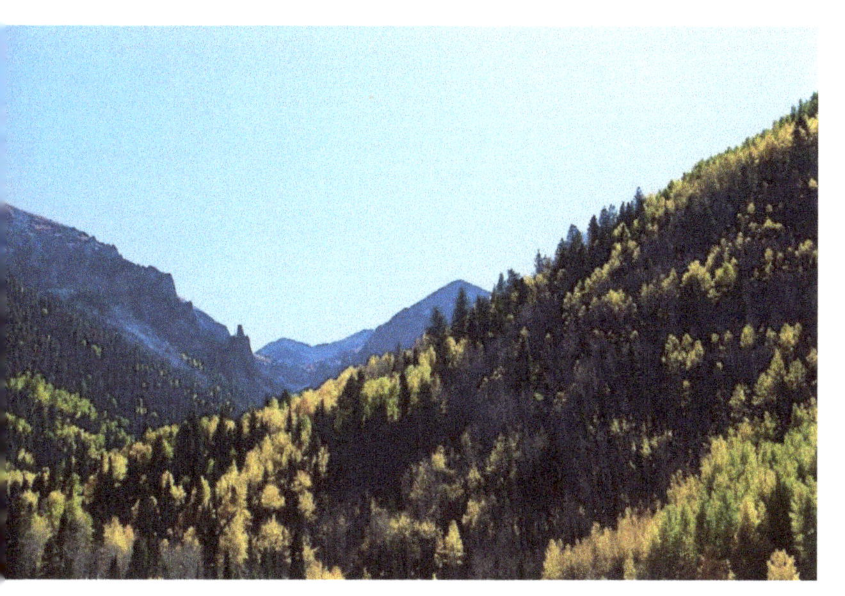

Grow

I've healed from everything before.

I have the power to heal from this, too.

Karma will come,

be patient.

Shoot for the stars and hope for the moon.

Where there is evil,

there is always good.

Life is so big,

yet so little at the same time.

There's a 99 percent chance that this

won't work out,

but there's a 1 percent chance it will,

and you're worth that one percent.

Having two homes will always fill and
break my heart.

"Time just wasn't on my side."

What a silly thing to say.

Time is a human constructed concept.

It doesn't even technically exist.

How can something that doesn't exist
not be on your side?

I see that as an excuse.

It wasn't time that wasn't on your side,

        some things just aren't meant to
work out,

                but you can't
            blame time for that.

I've always worried about being too
broken.

But isn't everyone at least a little bit
broken?

So maybe the secret is to not find
someone who can fix your broken parts,

but instead,

find someone who has broken parts
that fit with yours.

The moments where you feel lost are
the moments that are turning you into
the person you are supposed to be.

So much to look forward to,

yet so much to miss.

What a paradox of feelings.

The only thing left to do is to keep
moving forward.

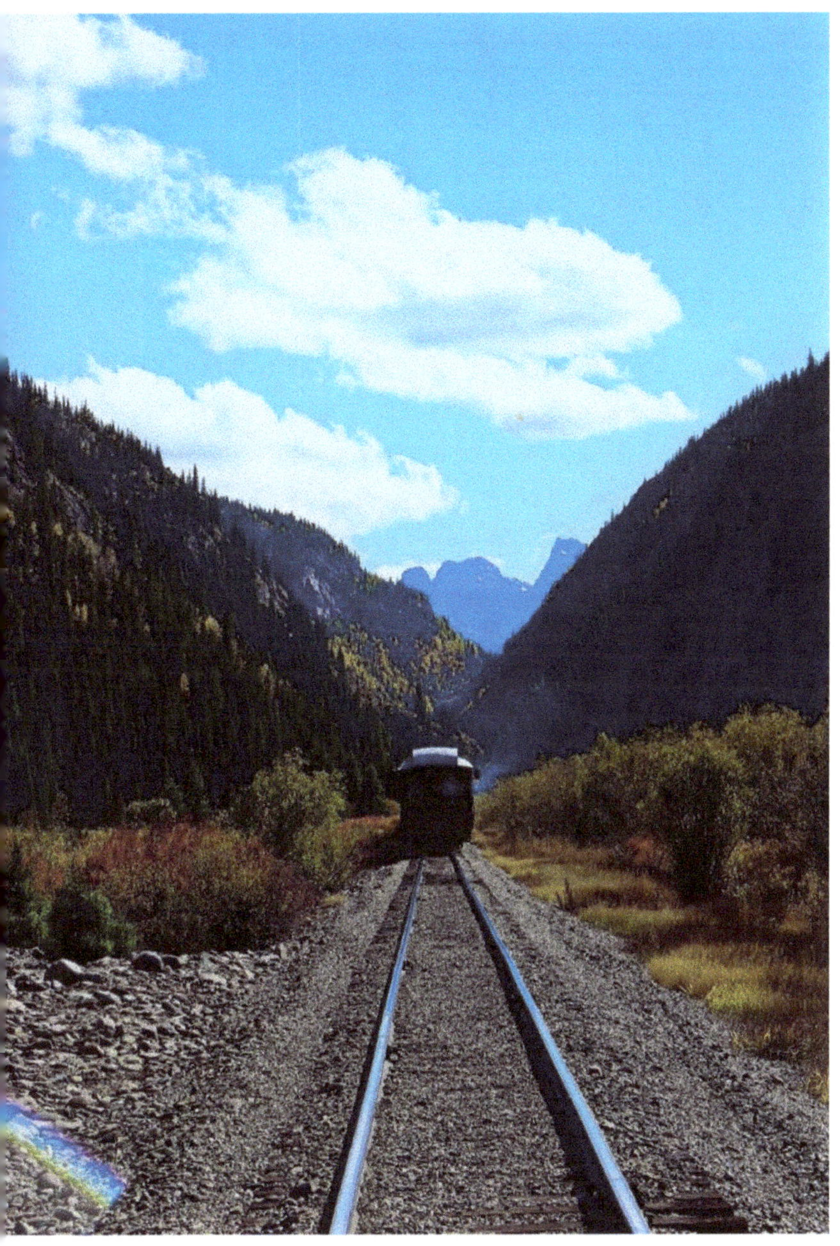

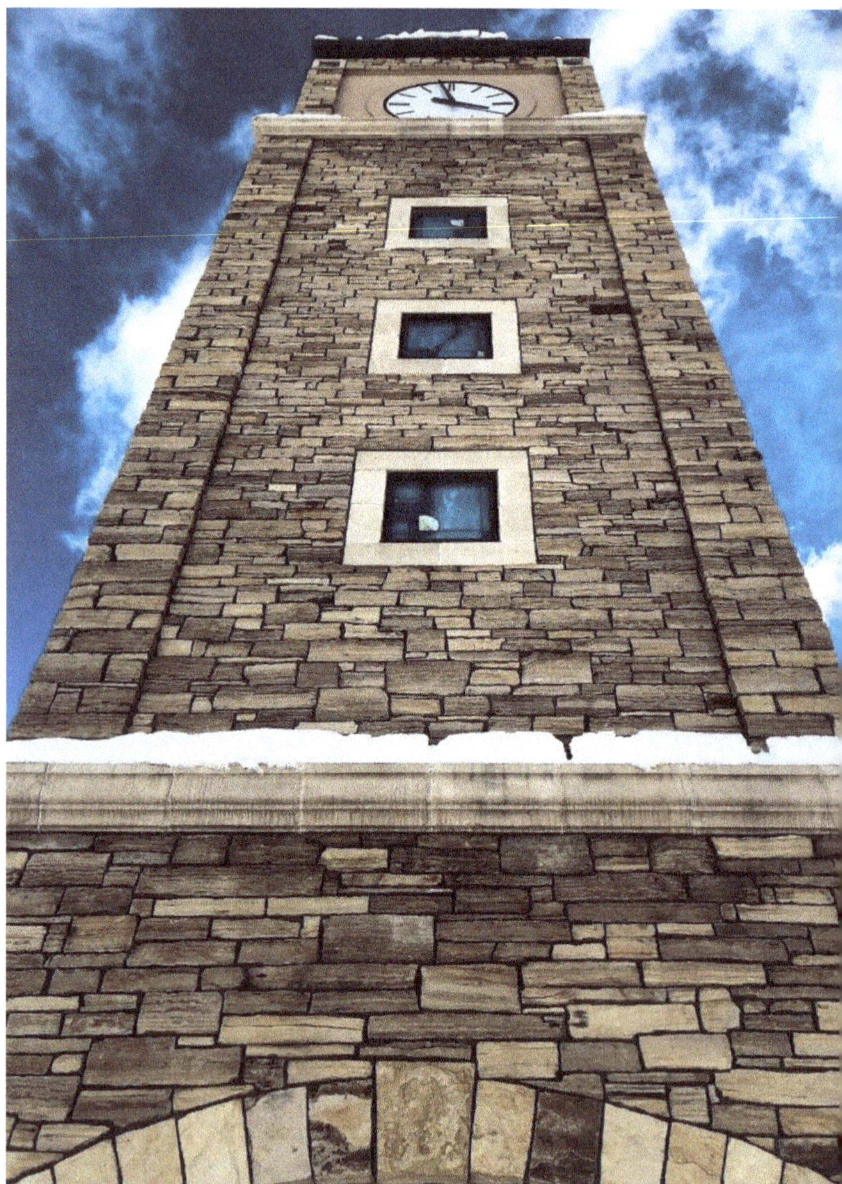

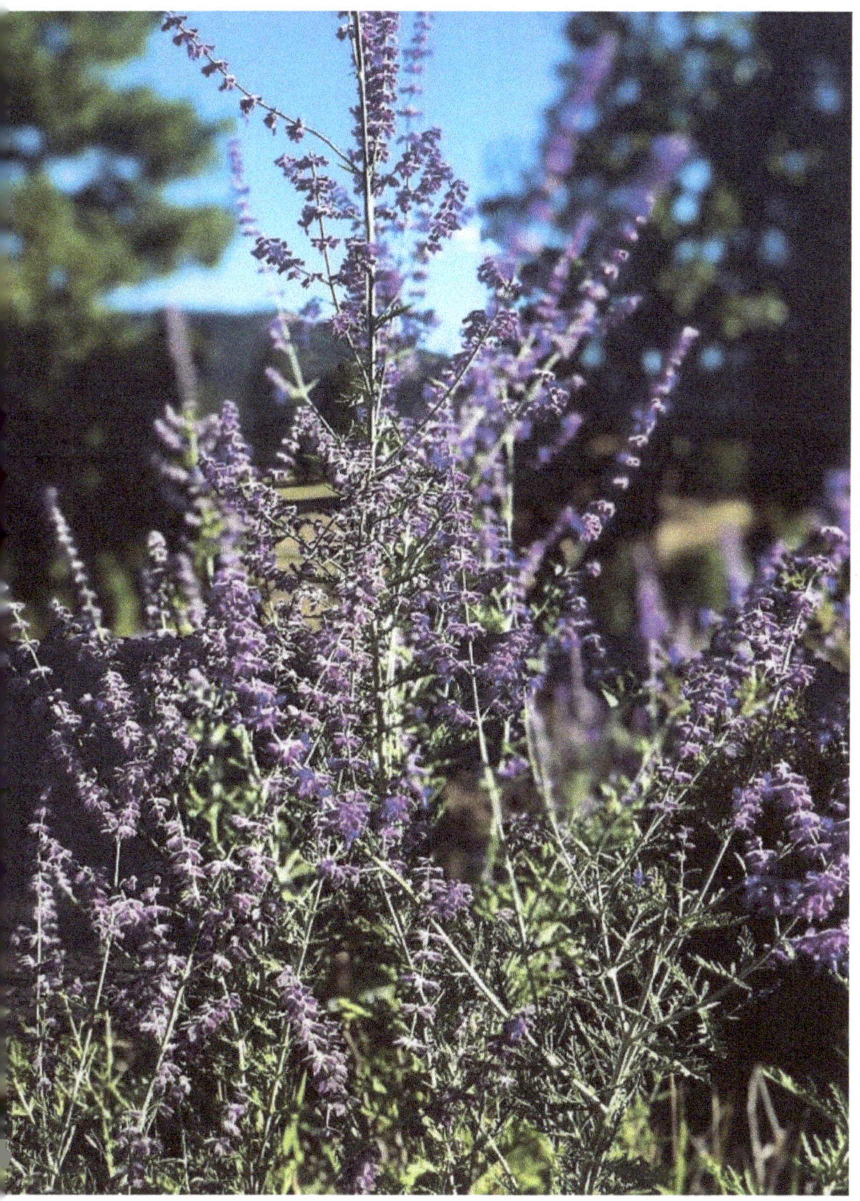

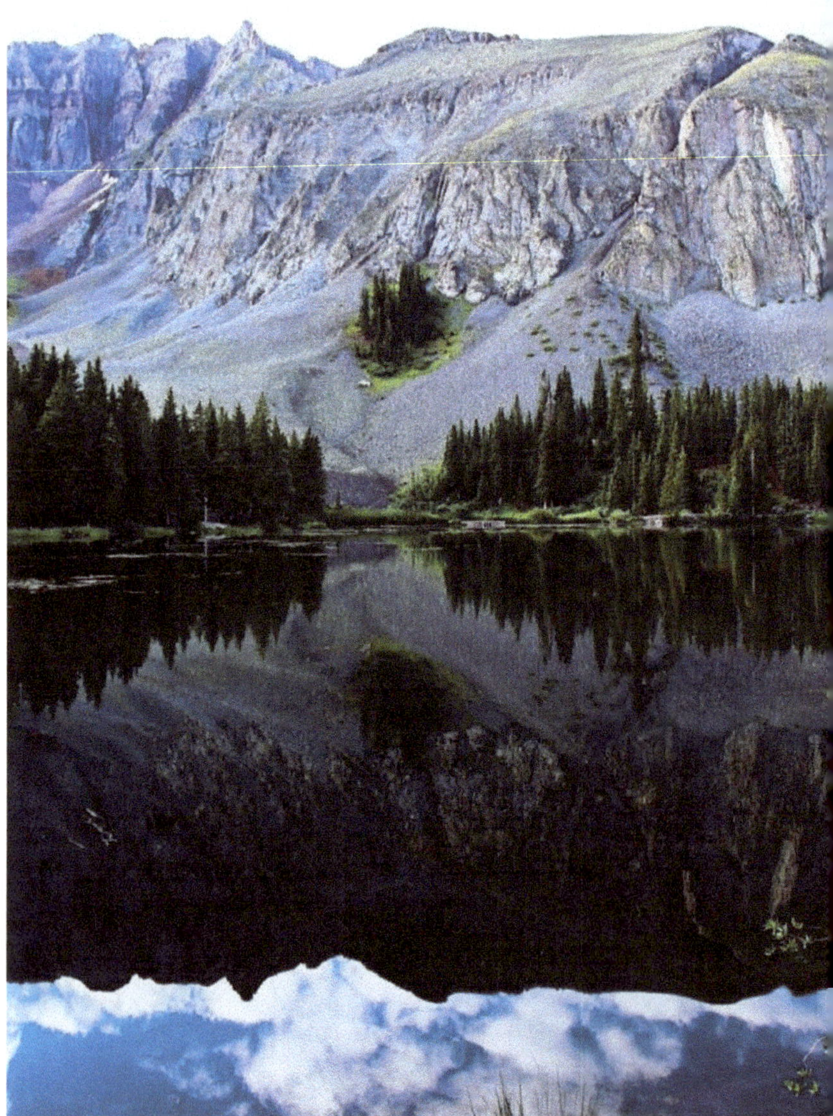

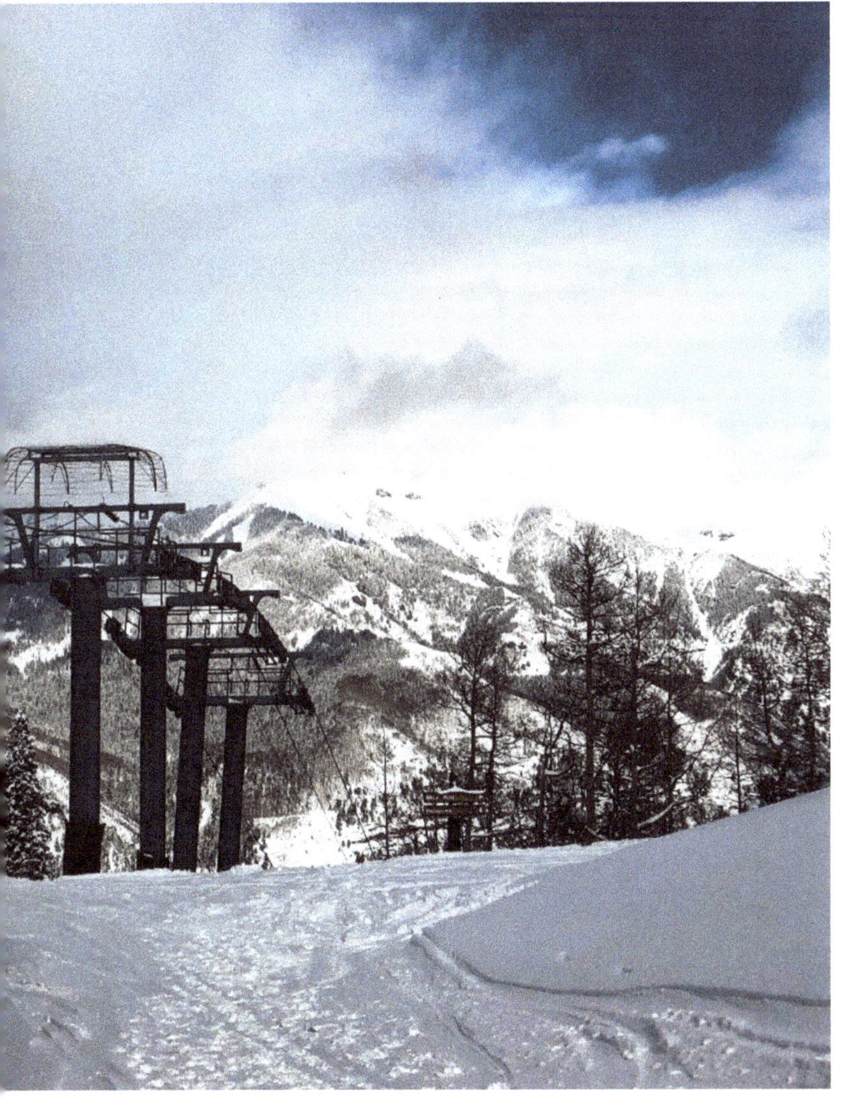

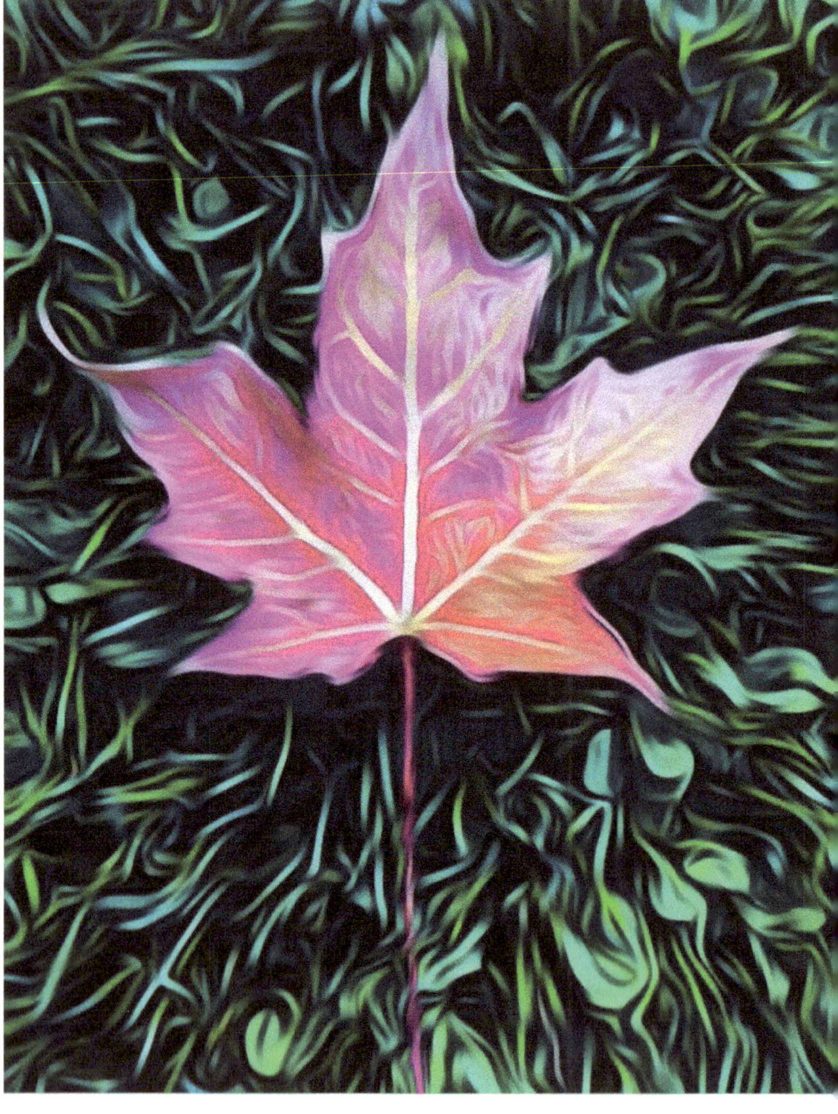

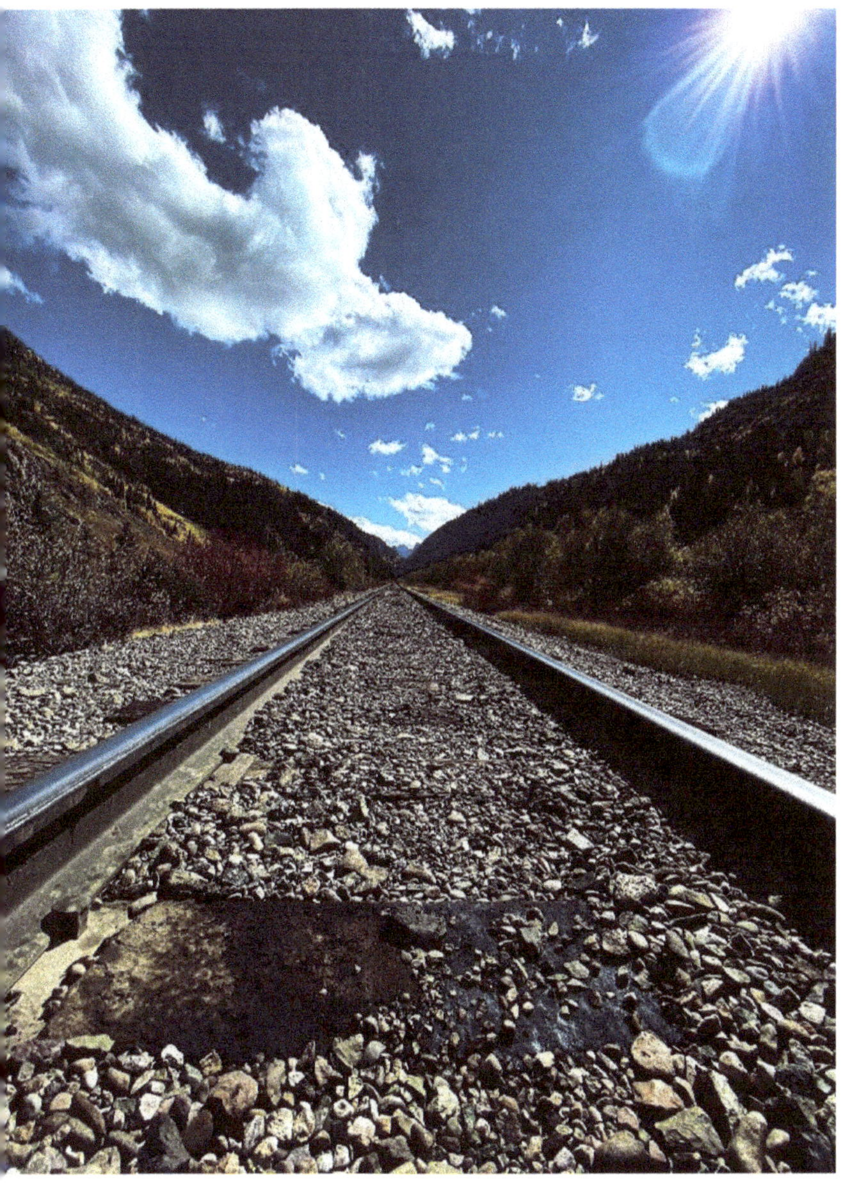

Wise Words from Mom

My mom has always given me amazing advice. I couldn't include all of the snippets of advice, but I have included the pieces of advice that I tend to remember the most.

"Always forgive.

Not for them,

but for you."

"I don't fire the first shot.

However,

    if they do,

        then they better duck."

"I used to not know if there was a god,
but every time I look at you,

I believe."

"Fireballs get thrown at other people, too."

-My mom reminding me bad things happen to other people, not just me.

"People make mistakes,

just like you have.

Be easy."

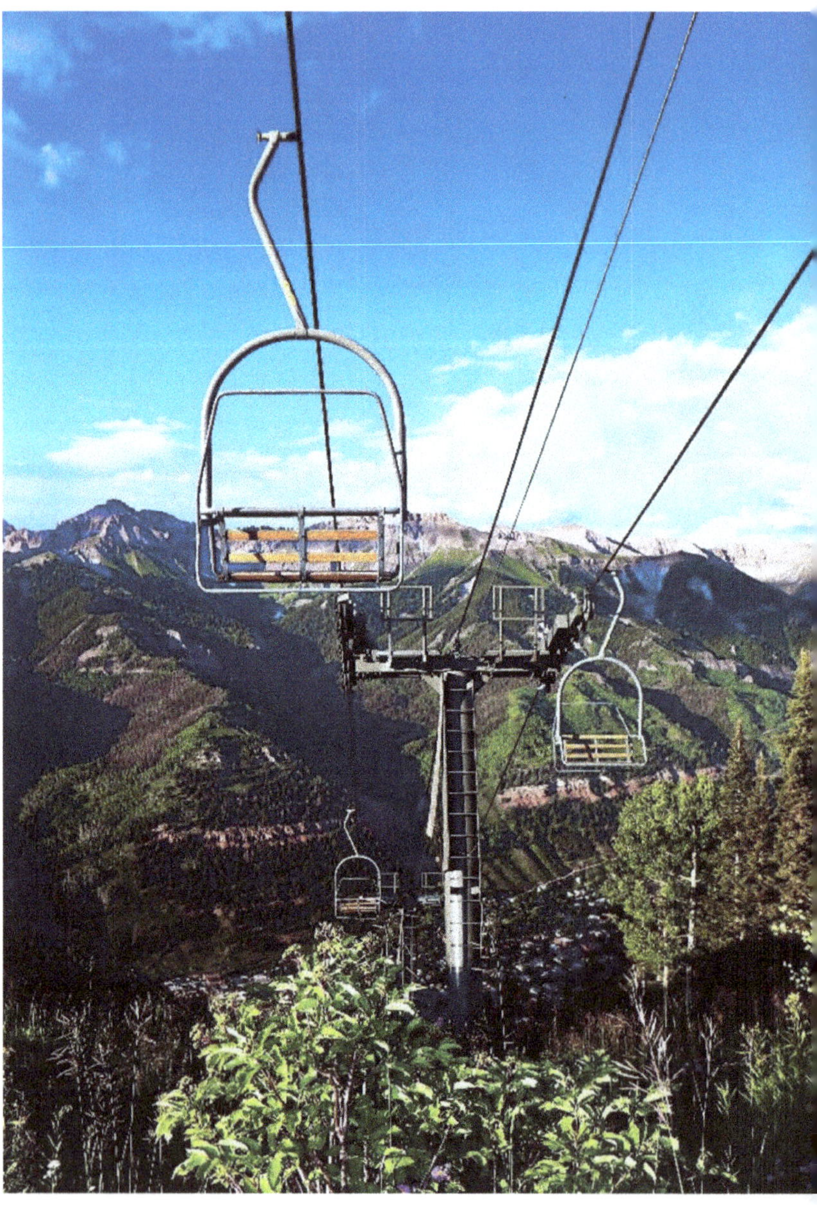

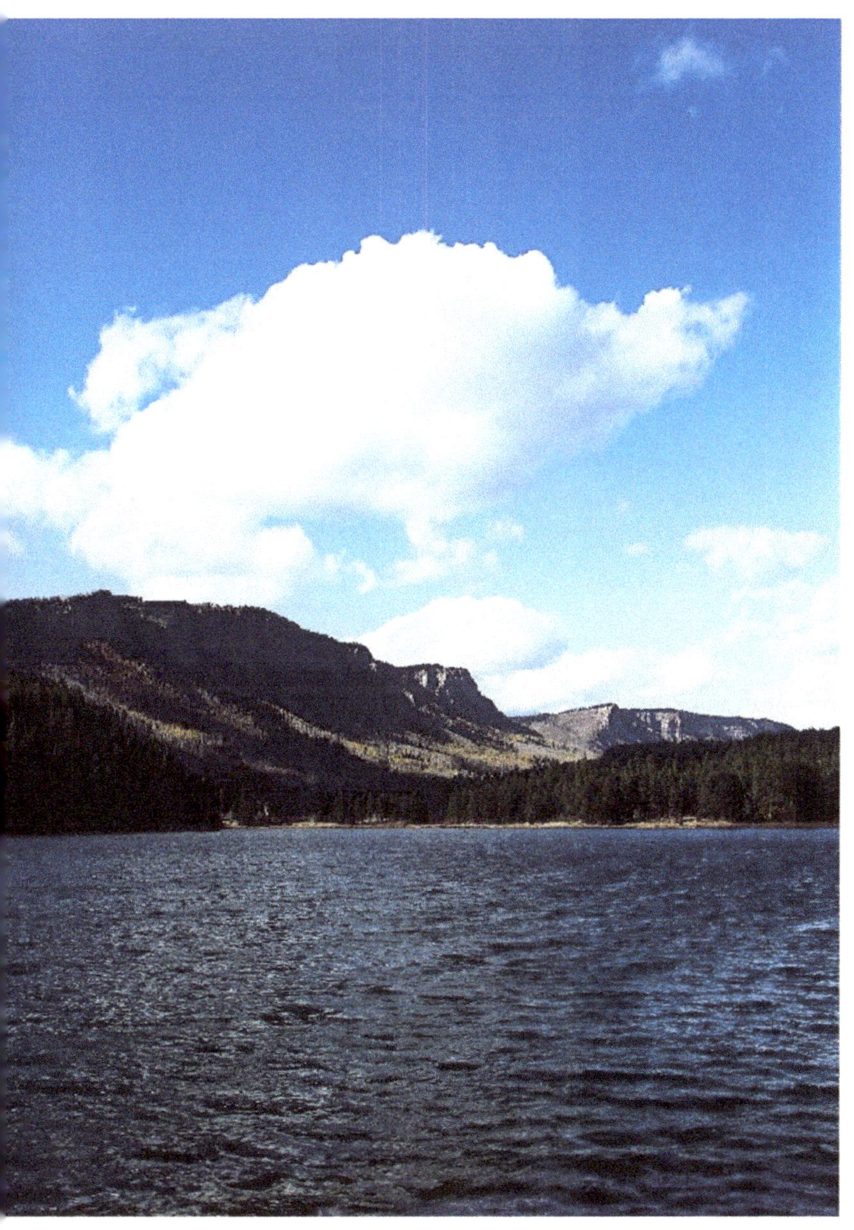

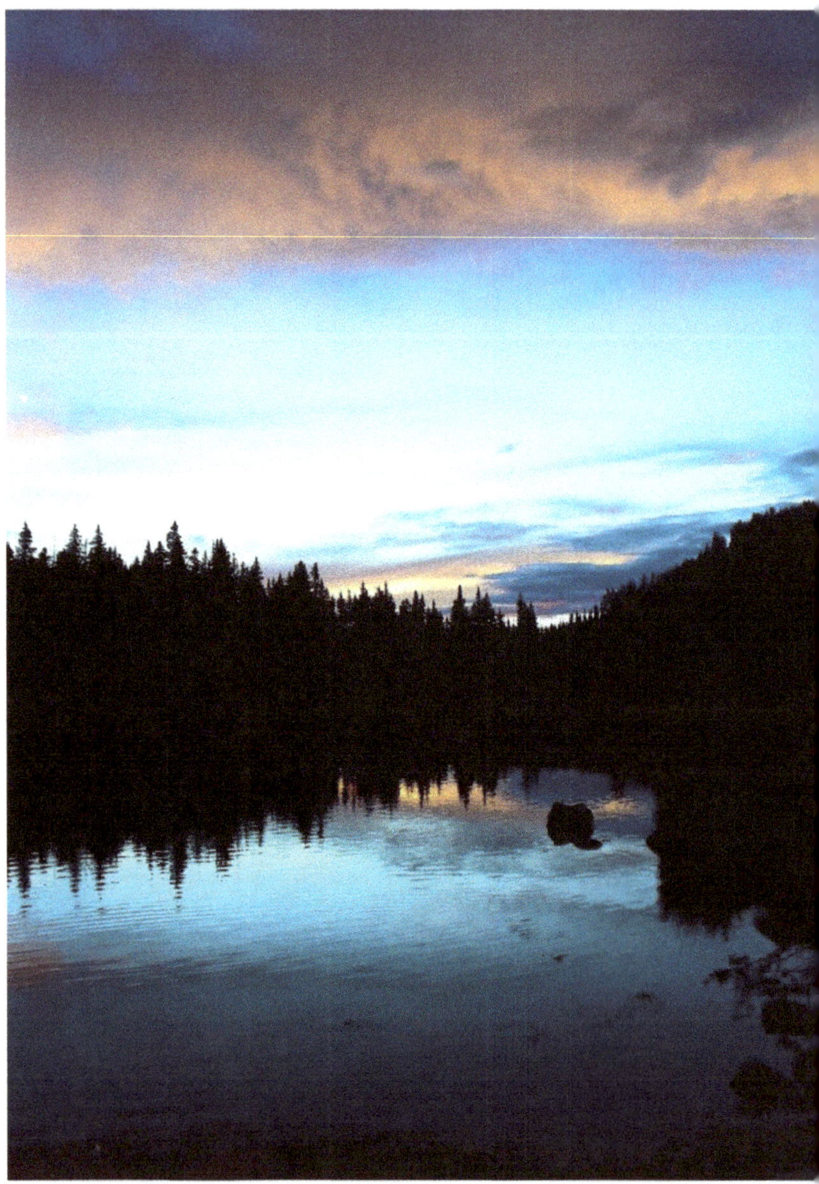

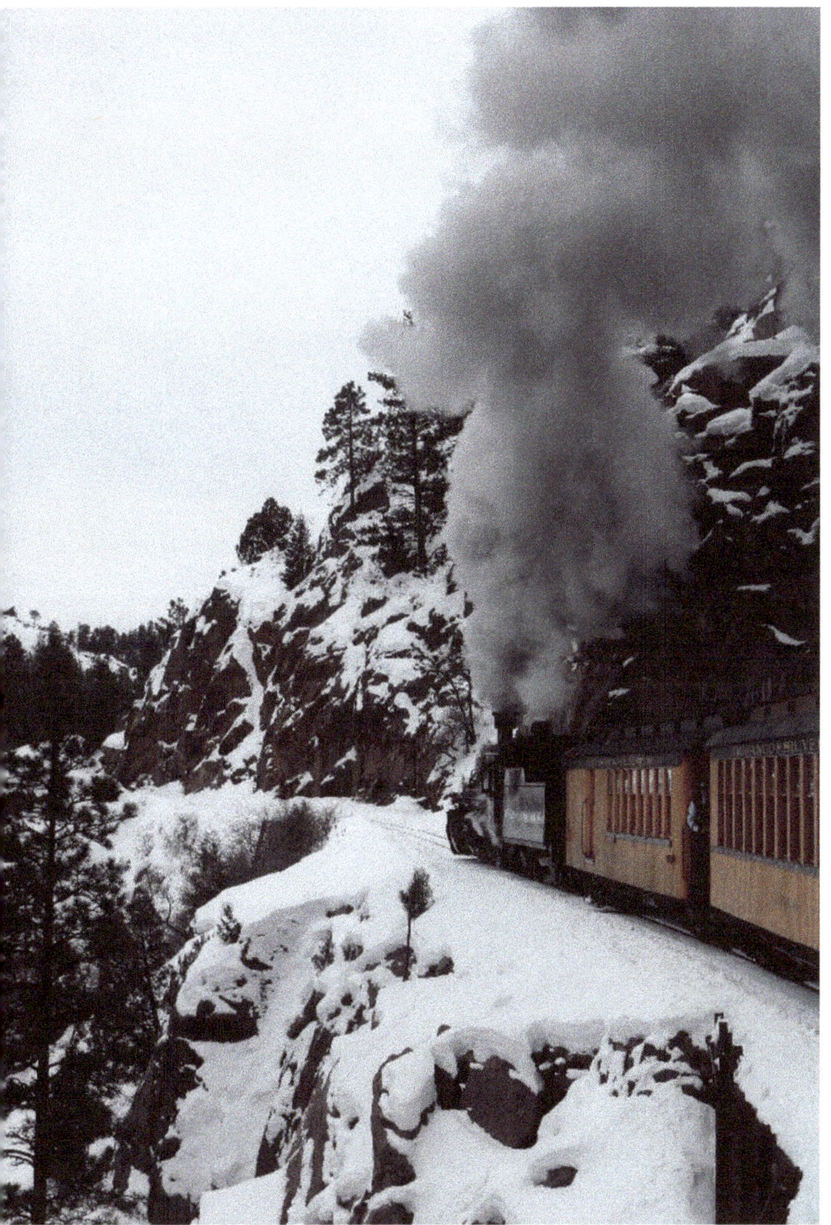

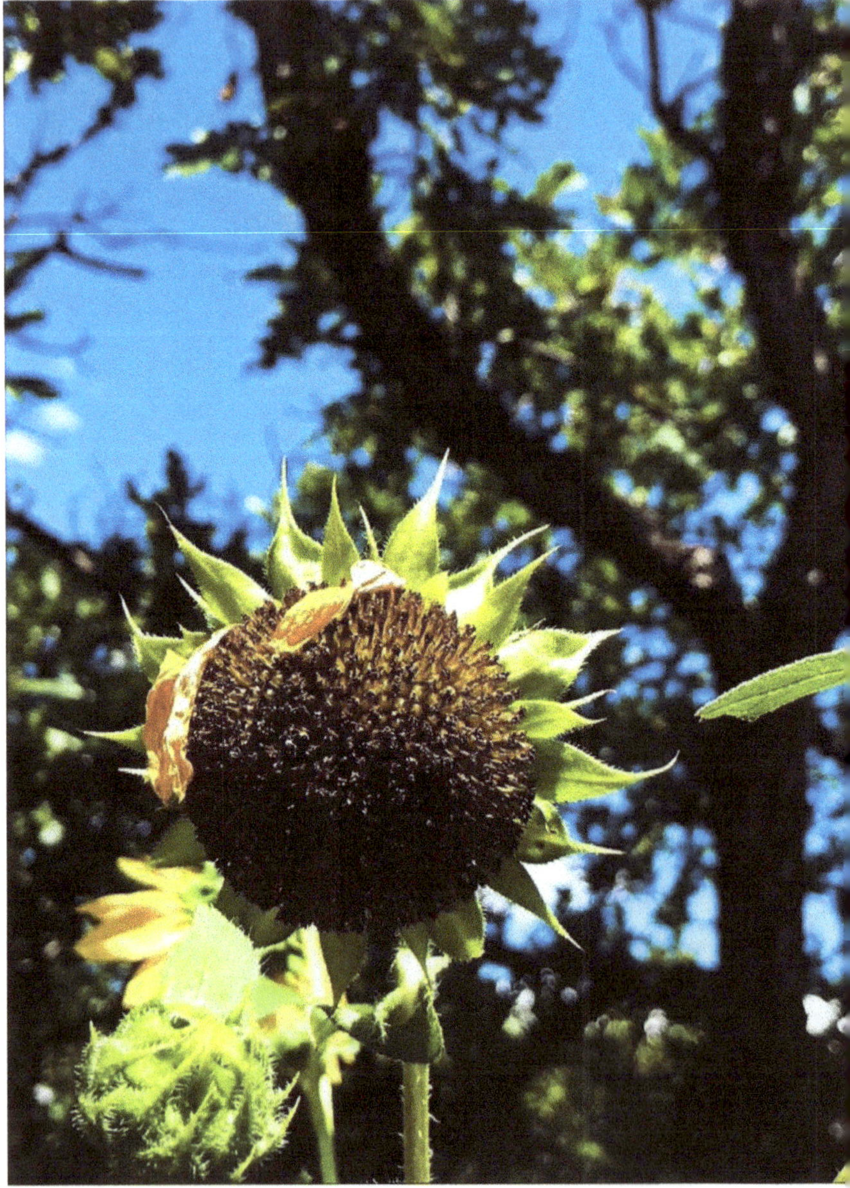

"Today I forgive myself. Not just once. Again, and again, and again. As many times as it takes to find peace."-
Anonymous

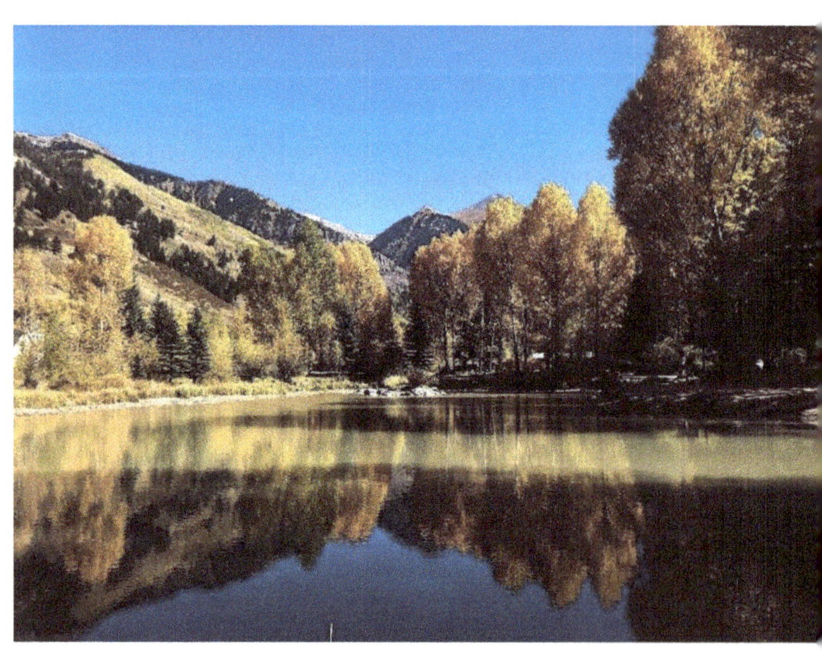

No matter how unbearable life gets, I promise you can make it through. Find people to love who love you back. Do good deeds. All the love you put out into the universe comes back to you, so never stop loving. Life has a lot to show you.

The views are worth it.

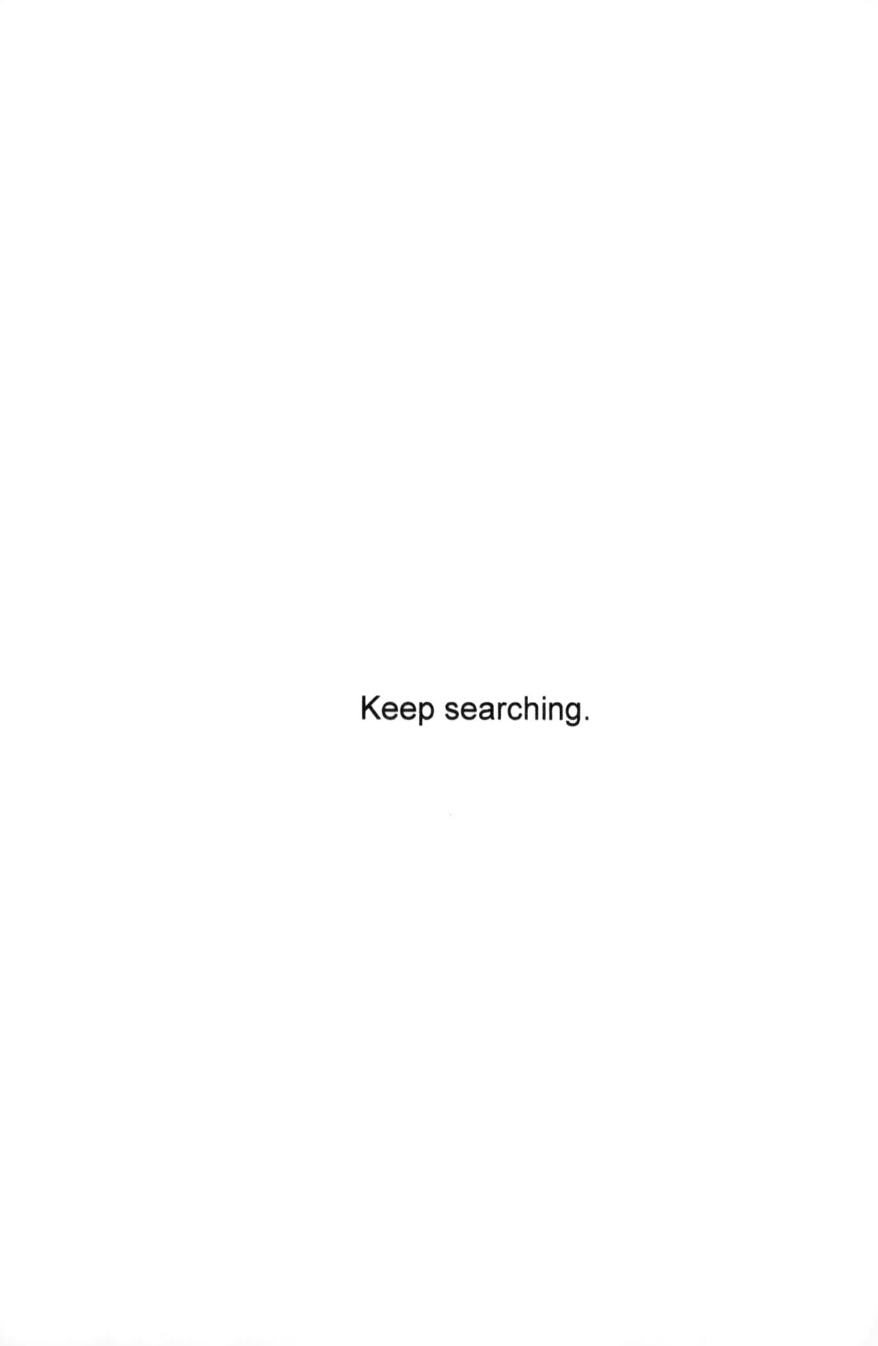
Keep searching.

And never forget...

You are so much stronger than you give
yourself credit for.

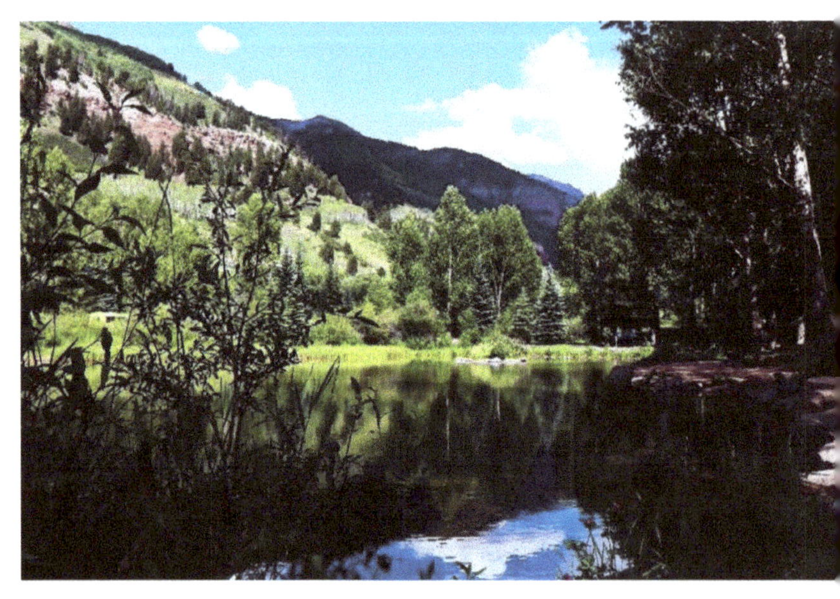

About the Author

Annie David

Annie is 21 years old, and grew up in Las Vegas, Nevada. Annie received her associate degree and high school diploma on the same day in 2017. She published a research paper on the effects of death and racism her senior year of college, and she graduated from Fort Lewis College in Durango, Colorado in 2019 with a bachelor's degree in psychology. Her main goal is to go to graduate school and become a psychologist in the near future.

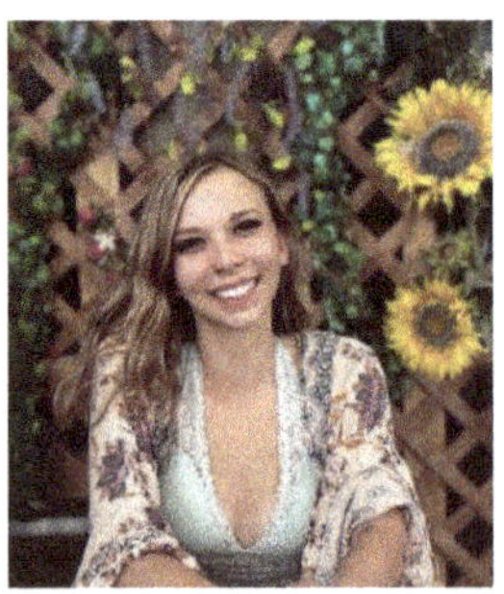